The Rhodesia Settlement, 1979-1980
An in-house study

The Rhodesia Settlement, 1979-1980
An in-house study

Edited by Patrick Salmon

Foreword by Lord Renwick of Clifton

Documents from the British Archives: No. 4

Documents from the British Archives: a thematic series with documents drawn from, or supplementing, volumes of *Documents on British Policy Overseas*, produced by the Foreign, Commonwealth and Development Office Historians.

Series editors: Patrick Salmon & Richard Smith

This publication is available online: www.issuu.com/fcohistorians

Cover illustration: Lancaster House
Credit: Gryffindor/Wikimedia Commons/Public Domain

ISBN: 9798548425638

CONTENTS

The Rhodesia Settlement: 1979-80

Part I: The Rhodesia Settlement

Part II: The Governor's Administration in Salisbury

LIST OF ILLUSTRATIONS

FOREWORD

Robin Renwick joined the Foreign Office in 1963. After serving in Dakar, New Delhi, Paris and in the Cabinet Office, he was Head of the Rhodesia Department, FCO, 1979-80; Political Adviser to the Governor of Rhodesia, 1980; Head of Chancery, Washington, 1981-84; Assistant Under-Secretary of State, FCO, 1984–87; Ambassador to South Africa, 1987-91; and Ambassador to the United States, 1991-95. He was created Baron Renwick of Clifton in 1997 and served as a cross-bench peer until 2018.

By the time Margaret Thatcher became Prime Minister in 1979, as she put it in her memoirs, Rhodesia had been a 'longstanding source of grief' to successive British governments. Labour and Conservative. Following Ian Smith's Unilateral Declaration of Independence in 1965, we had continued to have legal responsibility without even the vestige of any power. All previous attempts to find a solution had foundered on Smith's intransigence and that of the nationalist leaders, Nkomo and Mugabe. A conference in Geneva called by the Labour government had collapsed with not even the start of any serious negotiation.

At this point, it looked like a pretty hopeless cause. As the new head of the Rhodesia Department in the Foreign and Commonwealth Office, when I met Robert Mugabe in Mozambique, I was told flatly that he preferred war to negotiations and did not intend to engage in any. But the Permanent Under Secretary, Sir Michael Palliser, told us to come up with some new ideas. We were obliged to do so anyway, as Ian Smith had arranged a pseudo transfer of power to Bishop Muzorewa and the ensuing elections, without the parties of Nkomo and Mugabe, had been declared free and fair by the Conservative party's observer team.

1

As previous policies had failed anyway, we presented the new Conservative government, elected in May 1979, with an extremely risky plan, endorsed by Michael Palliser and his equally impressive deputy, a former submarine commander during the War, Sir Antony Duff. The new Foreign Secretary, Peter Carrington, and then the Prime Minister, were persuaded that the new Zimbabwe/Rhodesia constitution, which Margaret Thatcher subjected to forensic examination, did not represent real majority rule and that if we recognised the new regime, that would simply lead to an intensification of the war.

Peter Carrington and David Harlech having helped to convince the Prime Minister that simply recognising Muzorewa was an option that could lead only to further and worse problems, it was agreed instead that we should insist on changes to the new constitution, convene a conference in which no party would be permitted to block progress and then arrange elections supervised by us, in which all parties would be invited to participate, following which Rhodesia would be declared legally independent. The intention was to show that, this time, we meant business, which we never really had before.

Thatcher who, as she showed later in the Falklands, was a risk taker, liked the boldness of this plan and the astonishment with which it was greeted when presented to the Commonwealth leaders in Lusaka.

When the Lancaster House Conference convened, we presented a constitution which, indisputably, did provide for majority role and did not accept any amendments to it. For the transition, we insisted on a British Governor with full executive and legislative powers. The only serious negotiations were over the cease-fire, which took place each morning with the Rhodesian commanders and in the afternoon with those of the guerrilla forces. Brigadier Gurdon of the Ministry of Defence came up with a plan to achieve separation of the forces and Mugabe's military commander, Tongogara, proved far more interested in an agreement than his political master, as did Nkomo in his private meetings with us. But Mugabe's intention was to string out the Conference indefinitely. Summoned to see the Prime Minister, Peter Carrington and I had to tell her that unless we took the extremely risky step of despatching the Governor to Rhodesia before a cease-fire had been agreed, the Conference would never reach a conclusion.

The Conference ended apparently in failure, with Mugabe refusing to agree to anything and launching a viperish attack on us all. But we had befriended Fernando Honwana, the representative of President Samora Machel of Mozambique, who desperately needed an end to the war that had devastated his country. Fernando telephoned President Machel, who told Mugabe to sign the agreement or else he would receive no further

Mozambican support.

As Governor, Christopher Soames showed great courage in accepting his near impossible task. Cartoonists enjoyed depicting him having to be rescued by helicopter from the roof of Government House, as the Americans had been in Saigon. We passed some of the worst hours of our lives as small contingents of British soldiers were sent into remote and extremely dangerous rural areas to set up assembly places for the guerrilla forces. The cease-fire came within a hair's breadth of breaking down on several occasions and Ian Smith attempted to stage a revolt, only to be over-ruled by the Rhodesian commander, General Walls, and the head of intelligence, Ken Flower. We spent our days with one or other, or both of them. For Walls came under intense pressure from his troops and some of his colleagues to kick over the traces, but never did so, while Flower understood that the only alternative would be a disastrous end to the war.

Walls protested that half the numbers Mugabe had delivered to the assembly places were youths armed only with sticks. 'Any self respecting terrorist has an AK47!', he observed to me. Mugabe had kept back thousands of his troops to ensure that the villagers voted the right way. They engaged in a lot of intimidation, causing us to threaten to disqualify the worst affected areas from voting unless it diminished, which it then did. But the Rhodesian special forces had engaged in plenty of dirty tricks of their own, while South African military intelligence tried to blow up Mugabe.

When it came to the election, the UN representative, Perez de Cuellar, later Secretary General, was sufficiently impressed by the sight of British policeman in their shirt sleeves supervising the polling for him to declare the elections free and fair *before* the results were known, which few others were willing to do.

The result showed Nkomo winning all the seats in Matabeleland and Mugabe winning a massive majority against Muzorewa in all the Shona speaking provinces. We had expected Mugabe to win more votes than anyone else, though not to the extent he did.

The world press had more than half convinced themselves that we had been hoping to establish a government without Mugabe, though that would have led to an immediate resumption of the war. In reality our objective had to be to form a coalition government incorporating representatives of the Rhodesians, Nkomo and Mugabe, which was what we did. As Christopher Soames had promised him if he won the election, Mugabe was designated Prime Minister.

An appeal from General Walls to Thatcher to invalidate the election was dismissed forthwith. Duff and I were summoned to a crisis meeting with the Rhodesian commanders, at which Walls declared 'The enemy is about to become our government.'

We said that they would never have accepted our plan if they had not been losing the war. They could no longer protect the farmers. They had lost control of all the rural areas at night. Many of their own troops must have voted for Mugabe.

Turning to his colleagues, Walls said: 'You know that they are right.' The Rhodesian Light Infantry, which had been awaiting an order to revolt, were stood down. British troops started training the guerrillas to form the bulk of the Zimbabwe army.

I did not enjoy, any more than Margaret Thatcher did, handing Zimbabwe over to Robert Mugabe. But she was justifiably proud that, through what she described as 'muscular diplomacy'', we had stopped the war and brought Zimbabwe to legal independence and majority rule following an election under our supervision in far better circumstances than had looked remotely possible a year before.

Peter Carrington, rightly, has received much of the credit for the outcome, but this high wire performance would never have been possible without Margaret Thatcher's willingness to accept all the risks associated with it. Throughout the Conference, she flatly refused to meet Ian Smith because, unlike his supporters in her party, she did not forgive him his rebellion against the Crown and its disastrous consequences.

But at Lancaster House, Mugabe had kept telling me that 'power comes from the barrel of a gun' and 'I have a PhD in terrorism'. Having crushed a pseudo rebellion by Nkomo's supporters, he governed with relative moderation for two decades until his hold on power started to be threatened, at which point he reverted to the tactics of terror that he had relied on throughout the war. The white-owned farms were invaded by so-called war veterans and distributed to Mugabe associates, as were the proceeds of the diamond mines. The people of Zimbabwe were subjected to tyranny and a state of economic misery that has lasted ever since. It was Grace Mugabe's attempt to poison his successor, Emerson Mnangagwa, that led eventually to Mugabe's downfall in a military coup, but not to any relief for the people of Zimbabwe.

Years later, as I waited in Downing Street with the Prime Minister for the arrival of Nelson Mandela, she asked me if he was anything like Mugabe. I was able to assure her that I had never met two human beings less like each other than Robert Mugabe and Nelson Mandela.

ROBIN RENWICK

INTRODUCTION

No one was better qualified than Robin Renwick to tell the inside story of the Rhodesia Settlement: the constitutional conference at Lancaster House between September and December 1979 that brought an end to fourteen years of illegal white minority rule and a vicious civil war, and paved the way for the transition to free elections and the establishment of an independent Zimbabwe in February 1980.

As head of the Rhodesia Department at the Foreign and Commonwealth Office (FCO), Renwick had been a key member of the team led by Sir Antony Duff[1] and the Foreign Secretary, Lord Carrington, that had masterminded the Lancaster House process. During the conference he had been, along with his friend and colleague Charles Powell, the principal contact with the Popular Front leaders Joshua Nkomo and Robert Mugabe, meeting them almost daily in their London hotels. After the signature of the Lancaster House Agreement, Duff and Renwick became the most senior advisers to the British Governor-General, Christopher Soames, as he oversaw the fraught process of disarming the guerrilla armies and supervised the election campaign.

The idea of 'commissioning an in-house study of the Lancaster House Conference' was first formally suggested by Douglas Hurd, then a junior Foreign Office Minister, in May 1980. The thought had also occurred to the Permanent Under-Secretary (PUS) at the FCO, Sir Michael Palliser, who had suggested that such a study might be written by Sir Antony Duff.[2] In fact, however, the matter was already in hand, since Sir Antony and another senior FCO official, Derek Day, had lined Robin Renwick up for the job some time earlier. They had agreed that Renwick should spend four to six weeks reading the relevant papers in order to produce 'a comprehensive account of developments over Rhodesia since the present government came to power in May of last year, up to and including Zimbabwe independence'.[3] It was a solution pronounced 'excellent' by Palliser and 'very useful' by Hurd.[4] Renwick completed his account in late July 1980. It was divided into two parts, the first dealing with the Lancaster House negotiations, the second with the transfer of power in Rhodesia. Each part was

---

[1] Deputy Under-Secretary of State, FCO.
[2] Minute by Andrew Burns (Private Secretary to the PUS), 22 May 1980, p. 19 below.
[3] Minute by Derek Day (Assistant Under-Secretary for African Affairs), 27 May 1980, p. 20 below.
[4] Minutes of 27 and 28 May, ibid.

prefaced by a 'personal commentary': a concise overview in which Renwick outlined the key developments and issues as they appeared to him. The more detailed narrative, based on a close reading of the documents then followed.

'The Rhodesia Settlement: 1979-1980' was one of a number of in-house studies, sometimes termed 'internal histories', produced by Foreign Office officials from the early 1960s onwards. Sometimes they recorded a notably successful set of negotiations. Renwick's report clearly fell into this category, as did the precedent cited by Hurd, Sir Con O'Neill's report on the negotiations for Britain's entry into the European Economic Community in 1970-72.[5] Others recorded policy failures, including the very first such study, Rohan Butler's 'British Policy in the Relinquishment of Abadan in 1951', completed in 1962.[6] Another post-mortem, Nicholas Browne's report on British policy in Iran during the period leading up to the Iranian revolution, commissioned in 1979 by David Owen, Foreign Secretary in the previous Labour Government, was completed in April 1980, shortly before Renwick started work on his own.[7]

To a greater or lesser extent, all such studies were 'lessons learned' exercises. Yet most were kept highly confidential, usually given a high security classification and circulated to only a small number of officials. Sometimes, as in the case of the Browne report, knowledge spread by word of mouth: by the mid-1980s avoiding 'the Iranian mistake' was being cited as a reason for making contact with grassroots black opposition groups in South Africa.[8] This does not appear to have been the case with Renwick's study, even though it provided an object lesson in how to carry a high-risk strategy through to a successful conclusion. Moreover, unlike other such studies, it carried the stern injunction on its cover sheet that it must not 'be shown to Ministers of any administration other than the present one'. Copies therefore remained buried in the files until one was released to The National Archives (TNA) in 2012.[9] We welcome the opportunity to bring Robin Renwick's account of the Lancaster House Conference and its aftermath to a wider audience.

---

[5] Hurd had been Private Secretary to the Prime Minister, Edward Heath, at the time of the EEC negotiations.

[6] Two copies are available at TNA: FO 416/213 and FO 370/2694

[7] Again, two copies are available: TNA FCO 8/3601 and FCO 8/4029. The complete text has been archived by TNA at https://tinyurl.com/tyk7bjhc.

[8] *Documents on British Policy Overseas*, Series III, Vol. IX, *The Challenge of Apartheid: UK-South African Relations, 1985-1986* (London, 2017), p. 194.

[9] TNA FCO 106/430. The version published here is identical to the TNA copy except for a few minor corrections and the addition of photographs reproduced by kind permission of TNA and the Churchill Archives Centre, Cambridge.

Acknowledgements

I am grateful to Lord Renwick of Clifton for providing the foreword to this edition of his 1980 report; to the Rt Hon Sir Nicholas Soames and Edward Chaplin for their help in identifying the individuals in the photograph on page 119; to the staffs of The National Archives and the Churchill Archives Centre, Cambridge, for their assistance in providing the photographs. I also wish to thank my colleagues Sue Fleming and Paul Bali for their invaluable work in preparing the text for publication and compiling the lists of persons and abbreviations.

Credits

PATRICK SALMON

LIST OF PERSONS

Acland, Major General John Hugh Bevil, Military Adviser to the Governor of Rhodesia and Commander of the Commonwealth Monitoring Force; Chairman of the Ceasefire Commission
Allinson, Sir (Walter) Leonard, UK High Commissioner to Zambia
Allum, Peter Kevin, Rhodesian Police Commissioner
Anderson (Andersen), Chris, Rhodesian Minister of Justice to 11 December 1979

Banana, Reverend Canaan Sodindo, President of Zimbabwe, from 18 April 1980
Barnard, Major General Bert, Rhodesian Representative on the Ceasefire Commission
Botha, Pieter Willem, Prime Minister of South Africa, 1978-84
Botha, Pik, South African Foreign Minister
Boyd, Lord (Alan) (also known as Lennox-Boyd, Alan Tindall), British Conservative Peer; Secretary of State for the Colonies, 1954-1959
Boynton, Sir John Keyworth, Election Commissioner for the 1980 Rhodesian Election
Burns, Robert Andrew, Private Secretary to the Permanent Under-Secretary of State, FCO
Byatt, Ronald Archer Campbell, Assistant Under-Secretary of State for Africa, from August 1979

Carrington, Lord (Peter Alexander Rupert), UK Foreign Secretary, from 4 May 1979
Carter, (James) Jimmy Earl, President of the United States of America
Chambati, Ariston, ZAPU Secretary for Research; Joint-secretary for the Patriotic Front Delegation at Lancaster House
Cheysson, Claude, EEC Commissioner for Overseas Co-operation
Chidzero, Bernard Thomas Gibson, Zimbabwe Minister of Economic Planning and Development, from 19 April 1980
Chirau, Chief Jeremiah Sikireta, Leader of the Zimbabwe United People's Organisation
Chona, Mark, Special Adviser to President Kaunda
Cledwyn-Hughes, Lord (also known as Hughes, Cledwyn), British Labour politician and from July 1979 a Peer; HMG Special Envoy to Rhodesia from November 1978 to April 1979; Minister of State for Commonwealth Relations, 1964-66

Cronje, Rowan, Rhodesian Minister of Manpower and Social Affairs, 1977- 1 June 1979 and Rhodesian Minister of Education, 1978-1 June 1979; Rhodesian Deputy Minister of Lands, Natural Resources and Rural Development, 1 June 1979-12 December 1979

Dabengwa, Dumiso, Head of ZIPRA Intelligence
Day, Derek Malcolm, Assistant Under-Secretary of State, FCO; from February 1980, Deputy Under-Secretary of State for Africa
Duff, Sir Antony, Deputy Permanent Under-Secretary of State, FCO; Deputy Governor of Rhodesia, 12 December 1979-18 April 1980

Farndale, Major General Martin Baker, Director of Military Operations, MOD
Fifoot, Paul, Legal Adviser, FCO
Flower, Ken, Director of Rhodesian Central Intelligence Organisation
Fourie, Bernardus Gerhardus, Secretary of Foreign Affairs in the South African Foreign Ministry
Fraser, (John) Malcolm, Prime Minister of Australia
Fursdon, Major General Francis William Edward, Director of Military Assistance, MOD, 1977-1980

Gibbs, Sir Humphrey Vicary, Governor of Rhodesia, 1959-1969
Gilmour, Sir Ian Hedworth John Little, Lord Privy Seal, from 5 May 1979
Gurdon, Brigadier Adam, Chief of Staff for the Commonwealth Monitoring Force

Harlech, Lord (David) (also known as Ormsby-Gore, William David), British Conservative Peer; HMG Special Envoy to Africa, from 26 May 1979
Hawkins, Air Vice Marshal Harold, Rhodesian Diplomatic Representative in South Africa
Honwana, Fernando, Special Representative to President Machel
Hove, Byron Reuben Mtonhodzi, Zimbabwe Minister for the Public Service from 19 April 1980
Hurd, Douglas Richard, Minister of State, FCO, from 4 May 1979

Kamusikiri, Dr James, Private Secretary to Bishop Muzorewa
Kangai, Kumbirai, ZANU-PF Candidate for Manicaland, 1980 Rhodesian Election
Kaunda, Kenneth David, President of Zambia
Kissinger, Dr Henry Alfred, United States Secretary of State, 1973-77

Koornhof, Dr Pieter, South African Minister for Cooperation and Development

Leahy, John Henry Gladstone, UK Ambassador to South Africa, from July 1979
Luce, Richard Napier, Parliamentary Under-Secretary of State for Foreign Affairs, FCO, from 6 May 1979
Lyne, Roderic Michael John, Assistant Private Secretary to the Foreign Secretary, from September 1979

Macdonald, Hector Norman, Chief Justice of Rhodesia
McHenry, Donald Franchot, United States Ambassador and US Deputy Representative to the UN Security Council, 1977-79; United States Ambassador and Permanent Representative to the UN from September 1979 to 1981
McLaren, Air Marshal Michael John, Deputy Commander of Rhodesian Combined Operations
Machel, Samora, President of Mozambique
Malan, General Magnus Andre de Merindol, Chief of the South African Defence Force
Manley, Michael Norman, Prime Minister of Jamaica
Mnangagwa, Emerson Dambudzo, President of Zimbabwe, from 19 November 2017; Vice President of Zimbabwe, 2014-November 2017
Mugabe, Grace Ntombizodwa, First Lady of Zimbabwe, 1996-2017
Mugabe Robert Gabriel, Leader of ZANU and then ZANU-PF; First Prime Minister of Zimbabwe, from 18 April 1980
Mundawarara, Dr Silas, Deputy Prime Minister of Rhodesia, from 1 June 1979 to 11 December 1979
Muzenda, Simon Vengai, Zimbabwe Minister for Foreign Affairs, from 19 April 1980
Muzorewa, Bishop Abel Tendekayi, Leader of the UANC; Prime Minister of Rhodesia, from 1 June 1979-11 December 1979;

Ndiweni, Chief Kayisa, Leader of the United National Federal Party; Minister for Works in Bishop Muzorewa's Government
Nhongo, Rex (also known as Mujuru, Solomon), Commander and Chief of Operations of ZANLA
Nkala, Enos Mzombi Nkala, ZANU-PF Candidate, 1980 Rhodesian Election
Nkomo, Joshua Mqabuko Nyongolo, Leader of ZAPU; Zimbabwe Minister for Home Affairs, from 19 April 1980
Norbury, Brian, Principal Private Secretary to the UK Secretary of State

for Defence
Norman, Denis, Zimbabwe Minister of Agriculture from May 1980
Nyerere, President Julius Kambarage, President of Tanzania

Owen, Dr David Anthony Llewellyn, UK Foreign Secretary, 1977-1979

Palliser, Sir (Arthur) Michael, Permanent Under-Secretary, FCO
Parsons, Sir Anthony, UK Permanent Representative to the UN at UKMIS New York and UK Representative on the UN Security Council, from July 1979
Paul, Sir John Warburton, Former senior British colonial administrator; Lieutenant Governor of the Isle of Man, 1974-80
Perez de Cuellar, Javier Felipe Ricardo, UN Under-Secretary-General for Special Political Affairs
Perkins, Major General Kenneth, Director of Military Assistance, MOD, from April 1980
Powell, Charles David, Special Counsellor for Rhodesian negotiations 1979-80, FCO
Pym, Francis Leslie, UK Secretary of State for Defence from 4 May 1979

Ramphal, Sir Sonny (Shridath Surendranath), Commonwealth Secretary-General

Reilly, Brigadier Jeremy Calcott, Commander of 6th Field Force and UK Mobile Force, MOD
Renwick, Robin William, Head of Rhodesia Department; Adviser to the Governor of Rhodesia from 12 December 1979 to 18 April 1980

Sithole, Reverend Ndabaningi, Leader of the Zimbabwe African National Union-Ndonga party and member of Bishop Muzorewa's Government
Shann, (Keith Charles Owen) Mick, Former Australian Diplomat and Australian Representative of the Commonwealth Observers to Rhodesia
Smith, David Colville, Deputy Prime Minister of Rhodesia, 1976-79 and Minister of Finance, 1976-1979; Zimbabwe Minister of Trade and Commerce, from 19 April 1980
Smith, George, Secretary to the Rhodesian Cabinet
Smith, Ian Douglas, Prime Minister of Rhodesia, 1964 to 1 June 1979, Leader of the Rhodesian Front
Soames, Lord (Arthur) Christopher John, Lord President of the Council and Leader of the House of Lords, from 5 May 1979; Governor of Rhodesia, 12 December 1979-18 April 1980,

Thatcher, Margaret, UK Prime Minister, from 4 May 1979
Todd, Reverend (Reginald Stephen) Garfield, Prime Minister of Rhodesia, 1953-1958
Tongogara, General Josiah Magama, Commander of ZANLA until his death on 26 December 1979

Vance, Cyrus Robert, US Secretary of State, 1977- 28 April 1980
Van der Post, Colonel Laurens, Writer and explorer; unofficial adviser to Margaret Thatcher on Southern Africa
Vorster, John (Balthazar Johannes), Prime Minister of South Africa, 1966-78
Wales, Charles Philip Arthur George, HRH the Prince of Wales
Walls, Lieutenant General (George) Peter, Head of the Rhodesian Armed Forces and Head of Rhodesian Joint Operations Command

Young, David, Secretary to the Rhodesian Treasury

ABBREVIATIONS

ANC	African National Congress
AVM	Air Vice-Marshal
BBC	British Broadcasting Corporation
BP	British Petroleum
EEC	European Economic Community
ECGD	Export Credits Guarantee Department
FCO	Foreign and Commonwealth Office
FRELIMO	Liberation Front of Mozambique
HM	Her Majesty's
HMG	Her Majesty's Government
HRH	His Royal Highness
ICRC	International Committee of the Red Cross
MOD	Ministry of Defence
MP	Member of Parliament
NCO	Non-Commissioned Officer
NJOC	National Joint Operations Command
PAC	Pan Africanist Congress
PLO	Palestine Liberation Organisation
POLISARIO	Popular Front for the Liberation of Sagnia el-Hamra and Rio de Oro
SAANC	(South African) African National Congress
SWAPO	South West Africa People's Organisation
UANC	United African Council
UDI	Unilateral Declaration of Independence
UK	United Kingdom
UN	United Nations
UNHCR	United Nations High Commissioner for Refugees
US	United States
ZANLA	Zimbabwe African National Liberation Army
ZANU	Zimbabwe African National Union
ZANU-PF	Zimbabwe African National Union-Patriotic Front
ZAPU	Zimbabwe African People's Union
ZIPRA	Zimbabwe People's Revolutionary Army

THE DELEGATIONS

'NKOMO' (PATRIOTIC FRONT DELEGATION)

1. [unidentified]
2. [unidentified]
3. Ariston CHAMBATI
4. Jason MOYO
5. Daniel MADZIMBAMUTO
6. Willie MUSARURWA
7. Josiah CHINAMANO
8. Joshua NKOMO
9. Joseph MSIKA

Note: These photographs were taken at the beginning of the Lancaster House Conference to enable the United Kingdom delegation to identify members of the Patriotic Front and Salisbury delegations. Not all members of the delegations were present when the photographs were taken, and several identifications were lacking, incorrect or incomplete: these have been corrected where possible (Source: TNA, FCO 36/2463).

'MUGABE' (PATRIOTIC FRONT DELEGATION)

1. Robert MARERE
2. Kumbirai KANGAI
3. Dr Herbert USHEWOHKUNZE
4. Rugare GUMBO
5. Josiah TONGOGARA
6. Edgar TEKERE
7. Simon V. MUZENDA
8. Robert G. MUGABE
9. Mutuku HAMADZIRIPI

'MUZOREWA' (SALISBURY DELEGATION)

1. Rev Canaan BANANA
2. George NYANDORO
3. Dr Ahern PALLEY
4. James CHIKEREMA
5. Dr Elliot GABELLAH
6. Morton MALIANGA
7. Bishop A. MUZOREWA

Note: two seats have been left symbolically empty, one marking the absence of the ZANU leader Enos NKALA, the other that of Dr Edson SITHOLE, a lawyer and prominent supporter of Bishop Muzorewa (and cousin of the Rev Ndabaningi Sithole), who had been abducted in 1975 and whose body has never been found.

'SMITH' (SALISBURY DELEGATION)

1. Mark H. PARTRIDGE
2. David C. SMITH
3. Ian D. SMITH
4. Pieter K.F. VAN DER BYL
5. H.G. SQUIRES
6. John GILES
7. George SMITH
8. Jack GAYLARD
9. J. SNELL
10. D. MORRISON
11. Miss McLENNAN

'SITHOLE' (SALISBURY DELEGATION)

1. [unidentified]
2. Zuua MAKONI [probably D.C. MUKOME]
3. John SHONIWA
4, David ZAMCHIYA
5. Kenneth GWINDINGWI [pseudonym for John GWITIRA]
6. Ibbo MANDAZA
7. Kesiwe MALINDI
8. Rev Ndabaningi SITHOLE
9. Joseph H. MASANGOMAI

FCO MINUTES

Minute from Mr Burns (PS/PUS) to Mr Day, 22 May 1980

Mr Day,

Rhodesia: Lancaster House Conference

1. PS/Mr Hurd has told me that Mr Hurd is wondering whether there is any intention of commissioning an in-house study of the Lancaster House Conference.

2. I have mentioned this to the PUS who said the thought had occurred to him. He sees much attraction in the idea of a study of the Rhodesian independence process rather on the lines of the record which Sir Con O'Neill wrote on the Common Market entry negotiations. The Lancaster House Conference was a classical negotiation of its kind and its course should perhaps be recorded for posterity (though not necessarily for immediate publication) by someone who had been closely involved in it. The PUS wonders whether this would be a project which Sir Antony Duff might care to undertake with or without additional assistance. He would be grateful if you would consider this proposal, and, if you agree that Sir Antony Duff be approached, let him have a draft letter accordingly.

R.A. BURNS

cc: Mr Middleton (Research Department)
        Mr Braithwaite (Planning Staff)

Minute from Mr Day to Mr Burns, 27 May 1980

PS/PUS,

I discussed the need for some such record with Sir Antony Duff several weeks ago. We agreed that we should try to get a fairly comprehensive account of the Rhodesia negotiations down on paper. With the agreement of the Chief Clerk, Robin Renwick has been set to work on this. He will be spending the next four to six weeks going through the relevant papers and producing a comprehensive account of developments over Rhodesia since the present government came to power in May of last year, up to and including Zimbabwe independence.

2. I suggest that we might let this arrangement stand. When Mr Renwick has completed his record we could then arrange for copies to be sent to the other principal characters, including Sir A. Duff, to ensure that no vital elements have been omitted. I have no doubt that Mr Renwick will in any case keep in fairly close touch with Sir Antony whilst engaged in this work.

D.M. DAY

cc: Mr Middleton, Research Dept.
        Mr Braithwaite, Planning Staff

THE RHODESIA SETTLEMENT: 1979-1980

Covering Secret—UK Eyes A   Diplomatic Report No 185/81

NOTE

The Rhodesia Settlement: 1979-1980

The attached papers refer to the advice given to Ministers: and to the recommendations made by Lord Carrington to his Cabinet colleagues.

They may not, therefore, be shown to Ministers of any administration other than the present one

21 July 1980

Diplomatic Report 185/81

PART I

THE RHODESIA SETTLEMENT—PERSONAL COMMENTARY

1. The attached papers provide a history of the negotiations leading to the Rhodesia settlement. The following is a personal commentary.

2. In the early months of 1979 the chances for a negotiated settlement could hardly have looked worse. The Anglo-American proposals had run into fundamental objections from both sides. The requirement that the future Zimbabwe National Army should be 'based on the liberation forces' had deprived them of any chance of being accepted by the Salisbury parties and therefore of ever being implemented. President Carter had been talked into a commitment to this effect by President Nyerere. The Rhodesian authorities were not ready to accept a British Commissioner or a UN force. The Patriotic Front insisted that they must have a dominant role in any transitional administration, which must be based on their forces. Various adjustments were made to the Anglo-American proposals in an attempt to render them more acceptable to the Patriotic Front; but it was the Salisbury Government who were required to surrender power. The impression had been created that the British and American Governments would somehow know how to deliver the internal parties. Expectations were aroused that the proposals actually would be implemented. When it became apparent that they would not, African leaders understandably lost interest in them—except to the extent that they inhibited the British and American Governments from giving any encouragement to the internal settlement.

3. The prospects for direct negotiations did not look any more encouraging. Mr Smith's attempt in August 1978 to do a deal with Mr Nkomo was denounced by President Nyerere. Mr Nkomo, then as later, was fearful of entering into an agreement without Mr Mugabe. The possibility of further direct talks was destroyed by the shooting down of the Air Rhodesia Viscount at Kariba in September. Lord Cledwyn-Hughes had concluded that a conference at this time would have no chance of success. The Patriotic Front were convinced that they could achieve their aims by continuing the war. The Salisbury parties were determined to proceed with the internal settlement.

4. With the decline in the fortunes of Mr Smith, General Walls' role had become crucial. He did not see how our plans for an internationally supervised election could work. A UN force would not be able to cope

with the forces already on the ground inside Rhodesia. If the security forces were confined to barracks, the guerrillas would take over the local population. Mr Mugabe believed that if things continued as they were he had every chance of emerging as the winner in due course. Mr Nkomo's support seemed increasingly to be restricted to the minority Ndebele tribe. But ZIPRA had suffered heavily form the Rhodesian raids and some members of ZAPU were conscious that, if a negotiating opportunity were not taken, Mr Nkomo's chances thereafter could fade quickly.

5. Within Rhodesia the security situation had deteriorated steadily since 1976. The only areas not yet substantially affected by the war were Salisbury and Bulawayo. ZANLA (Mugabe) had committed a far higher proportion of their forces inside the country and their less conventional organisation rendered them less vulnerable to Rhodesian attacks than ZIPRA (Nkomo). Neither side was in sight of victory. The Patriotic Front had no capacity to confront the Rhodesian forces. Cross-border raids had inflicted considerable casualties on the guerrillas. But the whites were by now carrying an impossible burden of military service. Increasing numbers were deciding to leave (14,000 in 1978). There had been a decline since 1976 in industrial production. Employment was not expanding at a rate sufficient to absorb African school-leavers. The Patriotic Front were convinced they could win a war of attrition. The tide was running in their favour. In the short term, however, the war was likely to continue on its existing course, with the Rhodesians using pre-emptive strikes as a primary means of defence, guerrilla attacks on soft targets and the guerrillas, especially ZANLA, steadily extending their hold over the rural population.

6. The whole problem was rendered still more intractable by the constraints imposed by the Chapter VII determination and the juridical tangle which resulted from it. Rhodesia had long been a case of Britain being obliged to exercise responsibility without power. With a war now in progress it could reasonably be argued that it would be most unwise to get more directly involved. But if the situation deteriorated to the point of collapse (including the prospect of fighting between the two wings of the Patriotic Front), we faced the prospect of having to help to evacuate the 140,000 United Kingdom citizens and persons entitled to claim citizenship in Rhodesia. Contingency plans had been drawn up for such an eventuality. The only effective form of disengagement was to find a proper basis for the granting of legal independence; and to bring the country to independence in the best conditions we could achieve.

7. It had long been apparent that there was no possibility of agreement on the Anglo-American proposals, particularly in their elaborated form, and that a new basis for a settlement would have to be worked out. This would need to go back to the first principle underlying the original Anglo-

American proposals, i.e. that of impartially supervised elections. The difficulties of 'burying' the Anglo-American proposals were, however, considerable. The Government were committed to them. The State Department continued to regard them as well-nigh sacrosanct. They did offer a basis on which to maintain a comfortable position in the international community, to withhold recognition from the internal settlement and thereby maintain good relations with other African countries. But they could not contribute to a settlement of the problem either in terms of the situation in Rhodesia or of Britain's involvement in it.

8. The change of Government in May 1979 created the opportunity for a fresh approach in what was clearly going to be a final attack on the Rhodesia problem. The Government was determined to bring matters to a conclusion; and this created opportunities as well as dangers. There were in the early days strong pressures to grant independence to Bishop Muzorewa's Government. Mr Nkomo's blustering performances and Mr Mugabe's public commitment to a Marxist one-party state had done nothing to endear them to British opinion. Nkomo and the Zambians had suffered a series of military humiliations. Bishop Muzorewa seemed to be the only herbivore in the Rhodesian jungle. The turnout in the elections was impressive. Lord Boyd was a man of undoubted integrity and his report was bound to carry great weight with the Government and in the Conservative party. The Government came very close to the conclusion that the fifth principle was as close to having been fulfilled as it was ever likely to be.

9. It was clear from the outset, however, that if we recognised no other country except South Africa would follow suit. Mr Ian Smith had given the kiss of death to the chances of any African state doing so by his insistence on remaining in the Government. Recognition would have been followed by immediate requests for arms supplies and other forms of support in the war. The main concern of other western countries was with avoiding damage to their interests in the rest of Africa. We could not ourselves afford to allow our Rhodesia policy to be dictated elsewhere in Africa if we were ever to hope to achieve a solution. The absence of diplomatic relations with some of the more radical African Governments might not have been of great consequence to us. But we were liable to suffer serious economic damage in Nigeria and were concerned about the potential dangers to the British community in Zambia. Nor did the Government want to be accused of breaking up the Commonwealth or the Commonwealth meeting in Lusaka.

10. The Secretary of State was impressed by Lord Boyd's conclusions. But he was convinced that to have any prospect of success and of limiting the damage to our interests, we must seek to obtain a measure at least of

international support; it was obvious that this was no less essential to Rhodesia than to us. Lord Carrington also concluded that it would be very difficult to justify granting legal independence on the basis of a constitution which retained virtually all the levers of power in the hands of the whites.

11. The attitude of the Americans posed a particular problem. They remained attached to the Anglo-American proposals. They feared that the Conservative government would move towards recognition of the internal settlement and the effect this could have on their relations with the rest of Africa.

12. It was central to the new approach that this should be purely British initiative and not an Anglo-American enterprise. This was partly from necessity: the attitude of the Conservative Government to the problem was different to that of the Carter Administration. More fundamentally, however, the interminable processes which had been involved in consultations with the Americans on the Anglo-American proposals were liable to result in a real incapacity to take action at all. This was accentuated by the tendency of some of the US officials involved to unrealistic attitudes and a highly theoretical form of diplomacy. The urgency of the problem from our point of view was too great to continue on this basis.

13. But it was important to try to secure adequate US understanding for the policy we were now developing. Mr Vance, with undisguised relief, agreed that we should take the lead. In June President Carter announced the US Government's intention to maintain sanctions and managed to contain the Senate's efforts to overturn his decision. If in due course we lifted sanctions, it looked as if, under Congressional pressure, the United States would be obliged to follow suit. But they would not recognise the Muzorewa Government.

14. The Government concluded that the aim must be to bring Rhodesia to legal independence with the best start that was attainable, while limiting damage to our interests. But there could be no question of asking Parliament to renew sanctions in November. The obvious first step was to establish effective contact with Bishop Muzorewa, to try to win his confidence and to get ourselves into a position to exert real influence in Salisbury. From the outset Sir A. Duff emphasised to him the need to make an effort to wind down the war and achieve acceptance in Africa. Mr Day was appointed to maintain regular contact. Lord Harlech was an inspired choice to consult with the Commonwealth African Presidents. The Government announced its intention to build on the change which had taken place in Rhodesia to achieve a return to legality in conditions which secured wide international recognition.

15. The Nigerian government responded to Mr Day's appointment by placing an embargo on tenders from British firms for major government

contracts. The Nigerian attitude was a major problem throughout the early stages. The military government was intensely nationalistic and anxious to assert Nigeria's claims to leadership in Africa. The nationalisation of BP on the eve of the Commonwealth Conference was related to the supply of oil to South Africa, but was clearly intended also to indicate the kind of action the Nigerians and others might take if our Rhodesian policy was not to their liking.

16. Lord Harlech reported general criticism among the African Presidents of the constitution and a conviction that a solution must stem from Britain. There would also need to be some means of neutralising the claims of the Patriotic Front through a negotiation on the independence constitution, a test of acceptability and new elections or some combination of those elements. The Prime Minister told Bishop Muzorewa in July that the independence constitution would have to be comparable to the constitutions we had given to other African countries at independence. But if we regarded revised constitutional arrangements as acceptable, we would not permit them to be blocked by anyone else. It seems clear that the Bishop was prepared to consider constitutional change; but there would be strong resistance from the Rhodesian Front.

17. Before Lusaka, therefore, the Government had decided that it would call a constitutional conference but that it would not announce this until the Commonwealth meeting. An earlier announcement would have been pocketed by President Nyerere and others, who would then have resumed their attempts to prescribe the terms of a settlement. President Nyerere played a helpful role at Lusaka, not least because he still feared that we might recognise Bishop Muzorewa. The Prime Minister had already told the Bishop that there would have to be a test of acceptability, but the Government were not at this stage committed to new elections. This was agreed at Lusaka. As Lord Carrington reported to the Cabinet, elections were the natural corollary of a new constitution and a price worth paying to try to end the war.

18. The commitment to new elections brought a strong reaction from the South Africans, who were trying at this time to create a 'constellation' of well-disposed African states with close economic ties with them. Rhodesia, Botswana and, it was hoped, Namibia would eventually conform to the pattern. In June the South African Foreign Minister had visited London. Mr Pik Botha certainly hoped to establish some degree of ideological affinity with the Conservative Government. Apart from a shared concern about Soviet involvement in southern Africa, no such affinity really existed and Mr Botha's case was not helped by his hectoring manner. He argued that if we took the lead in recognising the Muzorewa Government much of Africa would follow suit; and in the same breath that the security

situation was so critical that if we did not lift sanctions immediately, Rhodesia would collapse.

19. The Rhodesians were more than ever dependent on South African military as well as financial support. It was essential at every stage to avoid their being confronted with a direct choice between co-operation with us and the continuance of South African assistance. This placed us on many occasions in an extremely difficult position. But the containment of this problem was essential to our ability to achieve a settlement at all. Sir A. Duff saw Mr P.W. Botha to urge the South Africans not to impede a settlement on the lines agreed at Lusaka.

20. We could also expect efforts to add to the Lusaka agreement and re-interpret it from the Commonwealth African Presidents. President Nyerere urged on us the need to act as the de-colonising power. He wondered how we could secure sufficient authority on the ground to supervise elections. The Prime Minister told him that we did indeed intend to act as the de-colonising power and to make clear the basis on which we believed agreement should be reached. The chances of success depended on the influence the Commonwealth African leaders were prepared to exert. The Patriotic Front had already rejected our constitutional proposals and elections held under our authority. 'Both sides', the Prime Minister wrote, 'will I hope realise that it is likely to be costly for them if they seek to frustrate a political solution on these lines'. The front-line presidents, especially President Machel, did make clear to the Patriotic Front leaders at the non-aligned conference in Havana that they expected them to negotiate seriously at Lancaster House. But Nyerere subsequently told the Prime Minister that he would not support a settlement unless it provided for the integration of the armed forces before elections were held. It was important to prevent him seeking once again to establish new conditions for a settlement and thereby under-cutting any chance of a successful negotiation. Presidents Kaunda and Machel proved to be more conscious of the practical impossibility of integrating the armies before elections.

21. In the run up to the Conference we worked out our negotiating tactics. It was clear that if we did not take a strong lead, we would get nowhere. Neither side was prepared to negotiate with the other. There was no prospect of achieving agreement by a process of dialogue between them. The Conference must not be allowed to develop into a replay of the fiasco in Geneva. We had in each phase to retain the initiative by putting forward British proposals, to deal firmly with procedural quibbles from the Patriotic Front and to make clear what the Government intended to recommend to Parliament as the basis for independence.

22. *The Government did not proceed on the assumption that a compre-*

hensive settlement was likely to be attainable. It would have been fool-hardy to do so. No previous attempt had ever got to the first stage of success. The Patriotic Front had invariably insisted on a dominant position in any transitional administration, which must be based on their forces. On the basis of the attitude they had adopted in previous negotiations, the chances of reaching agreement with them were not good, though Mr Nkomo would clearly be under more pressure to settle than Mr Mugabe. It seemed more probable that we should be able to agree an independence constitution with Bishop Muzorewa. It was clear that the objective, however, must be a comprehensive settlement. It was essential to play for success and to be seen to be doing so. If there was a breakdown the responsibility should be seen to rest with the Patriotic Front.

23. One lesson of the Anglo-American proposals was the futility of engaging in a negotiation with the Patriotic Front if they felt that, whatever their attitude, no sanctions would be applied to them. The strongest card in the Government's hand and the biggest single factor in favour of a settlement was the Government's readiness to state that if the Patriotic Front did not agree to reasonable terms, we would proceed without them. To make this threat credible, we had to mean it. The Government did not mean it and the Patriotic Front knew it. The objective was a solution with part at least of the Patriotic Front participating. The threat of a 'second-class' solution was crucial to our ability to achieve it, but at the outset the odds against a comprehensive settlement were high.

24. Vis-à-vis the Rhodesians we were aware of further appeals made by them in August to the South Africans for additional military assistance. Since the April elections the number of guerrillas inside the country had increased. The raids into Zambia had affected ZIPRA morale, but ZANLA were consolidating their hold on the rural areas. In the south east the Rhodesians estimated that for every guerrilla killed nine were reintroduced. It was difficult to carry out raids in Mozambique of the kind which had been effective in Zambia, though Rhodesian support for dissidents in western Mozambique increased President Machel's interest in a settlement. The Rhodesians pinned their hopes on the lifting of sanctions in November, but it was difficult to see how this could have much effect on the security situation. They were aware that time was not on their side but on that of the guerrillas and that—as they themselves put it—white emigration and the lowering of white morale, inadequate equipment and a declining economy put them on the losing side in the long term. Subsequently protestations by some of the Rhodesian commanders that they were 'let down' by us, that they could have got on top of the security situation or that the lifting of sanctions by Britain alone could have made a real impact on it should be seen in the light of their own estimate at the time that they were losing

the war. It was our assessment—and theirs—that this trend could only have been reversed or contained by massive external military assistance—or a weakening of support for the Patriotic Front by some at least of the neighbouring states and on the part of the local population.

25. This did mean that the Rhodesians had no option but to agree to whatever we proposed. This was never how the negotiations appeared at the time. They had given sufficient demonstrations of their capacity to reject negotiated solutions whatever the consequences for them. They could still try to force the partial lifting of sanctions in November by Britain and the US Congress and to get the South Africans more heavily committed to their support—and despite periodic threats to cut their losses, the South Africans were at this time increasing their military involvement. It was also open to the Rhodesians to raise the stakes in the war. This they were doing by carrying out increasingly unrestrained raids on the neighbouring countries. Before the April elections they had launched a series of successful attacks on guerrilla camps in Zambia and Mozambique and had attacked for the first time a ZIPRA camp in Angola. In March they organised the demolition of the oil depot in Beira. In April Rhodesian commandos destroyed the ZIPRA headquarters in Lusaka and Mr Nkomo's house, a stone's throw from that of President Kaunda. After being suspended during the Commonwealth Conference, raids into Zambia were resumed in August. In early September the Rhodesians launched a massive raid involving ground forces down the Limpopo valley. This was designed to pre-empt a ZANLA offensive during the constitutional conference but also to inflict substantial economic damage on Mozambique. They continued attacks on strategic targets in the neighbouring countries with the blowing up in October of a bridge carrying the only rail link between Zambia and Tanzania. On 5 November they interrupted the supply of maize to Zambia.

26. Nor would it have been wise to underestimate Mr Smith's capacity once again to destroy the chances of a settlement. We concluded that this did not mean we should be prepared to make a series of concessions to him. It would have been very damaging to permit the constitutional changes we were seeking to be whittled away or engage in a process of haggling about them. We had to be ready vis-à-vis both delegations to lay down clearly what we could accept and then to stick to it. It was clear that these tactics would require a display of political courage and a great deal of determination, as Mr Smith sought to push us up against the sanctions deadline, to appeal to his political sympathisers in Britain and to threaten to use the blocking power of the Rhodesian Front MPs under the existing Constitution to veto changes he disliked. It was therefore crucial before and during the Conference to seek the support and co-operation of the other leading members of the white community, in particular General

Walls, Mr David Smith and certain senior officials.

27. Mr Day had done much to prepare the ground in Salisbury, in particular in winning the confidence of African members of Bishop Muzorewa's delegation and in explaining our requirements on the central elements of the constitution. Intensive private consultations with key members of the Rhodesian delegation were engaged as soon as they arrived in London. The Cabinet Secretary and some other senior officials took the line that there could be no change in the blocking mechanism. They were told that in that event there would be no settlement. The Director of the Rhodesian Central Intelligence Organisation, Mr Flower, and the Rhodesian Representative in South Africa, Air Vice Marshal Hawkins, proved to be useful allies. They realised that the deterioration of the security situation could only be arrested by seizing the opportunity to reach a political settlement. They were, however, thinking in terms of a settlement with Britain and not of the participation of any part of the Patriotic Front. They made it clear from the outset that the breaking point for them and for the military commanders would be any reversion to the ideas in the Anglo-American proposals involving interference with the security forces.

28. Against this background our tactics at each stage had to be ourselves to draw the line on which agreement could in theory be reached; and then to push the Salisbury delegation as hard as we could into acceptance of it so that whatever was on offer in the Conference was a real offer, capable of being implemented. This meant that the real negotiating battles with the Salisbury delegation had to be fought out in private. It required no less effort and determination to secure successively their acceptance of a satisfactory constitution, new elections, the surrender of power to a British Governor and workable arrangements for the cease-fire than to force the Patriotic Front over the hurdles of acceptance of those same requirements. In private arguments with the Salisbury delegation and public confrontations with the Patriotic Front we were assisted by the fact that neither delegation was able to maintain more than a semblance of unity. Several members of the Rhodesian delegation were conscious that this was indeed the last chance while the Patriotic Front realised that, for the first time, they too were liable to face real penalties if they did not agree. We were able to bring home to both sides that this was not another round of 'all-party discussions', but a serious and final negotiation.

29. In the Conference we developed a 'building block' approach. In each phase our initial outline proposals were so general as to render it difficult for either side reasonably to object to them. Having wrung agreement out of the Salisbury delegation we would then table proposals which, for all their disadvantages in Patriotic Front's eyes, carried the very real advantage—which they could appreciate—that we could implement them;

and they knew that we were in any event determined to do so. The purpose of tackling the constitution first was to underline the difference between this and any previous meeting; to emphasise its finality; to give the Conference a clear focus; and, if we could achieve a reasonable constitution, to demonstrate that the war was no longer about majority rule.

30. The negotiations on the constitution involved a good deal of pressure on the Salisbury delegation including the revelation that not all sanctions would lapse automatically on 15 November. We benefitted greatly from the fact that Mr Smith was no longer in control but, at the outset, he continued to exert a hypnotic influence over other members of the delegation, who were afraid of him. The first month of the Conference was devoted to breaking his hold on the Salisbury delegation and getting them to accept a reasonable constitution. Far from being the easiest, this was one of the most difficult phases of the Conference. But after long and difficult bilateral negotiations we were able to achieve an independence constitution which in all respects we could defend in Parliament and elsewhere. Mr Smith's attempt to appeal to white opinion in Salisbury and to the military commanders to reject our proposals was unsuccessful: Mr Flower had returned to Salisbury to brief his colleagues in favour of them.

31. We then had to work long and hard on the individual members of the Salisbury delegation to persuade them to announce their acceptance of new elections. There was strong resistance within the delegation and the South Africans were advising the Bishop not to agree. In announcing his intention to do so, Muzorewa told his delegation that it was he who had most to lose: there was no guarantee that he would win new elections. He proceeded throughout on the assumption that the Patriotic Front were going to participate and never wavered in that opinion. At the same time efforts were made in informal contacts by the Lord Privy Seal and others to convince the Patriotic Front that we were genuinely trying to achieve a settlement in which they could participate. These approaches met with a more positive response from ZAPU than from ZANU.

32. The Patriotic Front's objections were gradually whittled away as they accepted a constitutional Presidency and the white seats in the Assembly (with ZANU agreeing to this under pressure from President Machel). They argued that the Conference should proceed to the transitional arrangements, but maintained their reservations on land, pensions, the army, police, public service, judiciary, etc. We tried to help them over their difficulties with an offer of help with schemes for agricultural development. But Lord Carrington told the Conservative Party Conference that no-one would be allowed to decide unilaterally that Rhodesia should continue in illegality and isolation. We were determined not to allow the Patriotic Front to maintain reservations on the constitution before proceeding

to the next stage. We had to insist that the negotiations should proceed stage by stage and not degenerate into another round of all-party talks. It was no less essential to obtain an unequivocal response if we were to avoid serious difficulties with and for Bishop Muzorewa.

33. There were by this time strong indications that Nkomo and ZAPU were anxious to come to an agreement and that some of the front-line Presidents felt that our constitutional proposals provided for genuine majority rule and should be accepted. In an effort to force the Patriotic Front over this hurdle—and in order to retain the confidence of the Salisbury delegation—Lord Carrington announced on 15 October that in view of the Patriotic Front's failure to accept the constitution, discussions about the arrangements to implement it would take place without their participation; but it would be open to them to participate as soon as they could indicate acceptance. The Commonwealth Secretary General criticised our action—but busied himself with seeking a formula to enable the Patriotic Front to agree. Three days later the Patriotic Front accepted, subject to agreement on the transitional arrangements. The tactics we had adopted over the constitution—the struggle to win the agreement of the Salisbury delegation, the gradual elaboration of our proposals, marginal concessions to the Patriotic Front and a final ultimatum to get them to accept—were to be repeated in the other phases of the Conference.

34. The next step was to work for a return to legality. The question was whether we should aim for this with the British Governor assuming direct legislative and executive authority; or while leaving the existing Government in place with our role confined to the supervision of the elections. The Lusaka agreement—that elections should be supervised under our authority—was in theory susceptible to either interpretation. It was clear, however; that the only arrangements which would carry conviction with the front-line Presidents and the international community would be a British Governor with executive authority. This was also the only firm basis in international law for a return to legality—despite the fact that we had never exercised direct responsibility for Rhodesia before. As over the constitution, it was essential to retain the initiative and proceed on the basis of a firm British plan.

35. There began a long and very difficult process of negotiations with the Salisbury delegation. We had already begun to discuss some of these ideas with those with whom we had formed a close working relationship (Dr Mundawarara, Dr Kamusikiri, Mr David Smith, Mr Flower and AVM Hawkins). But the Rhodesian military commanders were adamantly opposed to Bishop Muzorewa giving up his position as Prime Minister. They wanted us to appoint a Governor-General and supervise the elections, leaving the existing Government in place. The South African were indicating

that if Bishop Muzorewa stood aside, they might withdraw their military support. Most of the Bishop's African colleagues were no less strongly oppose to standing down. Bishop Muzorewa went through a long period of uncertainty before reaching a decision. Privately he asked Lord Carrington to tell his delegation formally that, unless certain indispensable steps were taken, international recognition would not be forthcoming and the war would continue and intensify. Lord Carrington told the Salisbury delegation that there would have to be a British Governor exercising control. This was the only basis on which we could carry our friends with us and demonstrate that the elections we were organising were free and fair.

36. Mr Pik Botha had returned to London. It was more than ever necessary to carry the South Africans with us. The Prime Minister explained our position and Mr Botha was persuaded by her and by General Walls not to impede a settlement on this basis. The South Africans and General Walls were assured that we would not interrupt supplies of South African military equipment. In addition to the regular contacts through Mr Leahy, Colonel Laurens Van Der Post helped to keep the South African Government informed, through Dr Koornhof, of our approach. His efforts contributed to their acceptance of it.

37. In the second phase we had decided to put forward transitional proposals which were radically simplified in relation to the Anglo-American proposals and to insist on a very short transitional period with responsibility for the administration remaining exclusively in the hands of the Governor. This was because we believed that if we were to implement an agreement, there was a chance of success on this basis and not with any more elaborate scheme. There was no practical alternative to assuming control of the existing police and administration. Nor would any alternative proposal have been accepted by the Salisbury Government.

38. In the Conference Lord Carrington rejected the Patriotic Front's demand for a six month interim period, with a governing council, a UN peace-keeping force, a UN police force and the re-organisation of the army, police, judiciary and civil service before elections. A short transitional period was crucial. The Salisbury delegation were strongly opposed to a longer period. More fundamentally, however, so were we. If agreement could be reached, we would face the task of assuming direct responsibility for Rhodesia in a very difficult military and political situation. The longer the transitional period the greater the chances of a breakdown of the cease-fire, whether for military reasons or because one side or the other saw the tide turning against them. The only way to ensure that the political leaders were unable constantly to seek to interfere in the running of the country and thereby render the Governor's task impossible was to oblige

them to commit themselves forthwith to the election campaign. Neverthe-less, the Patriotic Front's demands for a longer period found a good deal of sympathy among countries who would not themselves have to bear any part of the responsibility for what happened in this period. As President Nyerere lobbied Government after Government we were subjected to a good deal of gratuitous advice. We pointed out that we alone would be responsible for the administration of Rhodesia; and that we were not pre-pared to accept that responsibility for longer than was strictly necessary to carry out the task we would be undertaking.

39. Bishop Muzorewa was still undecided about standing aside. Lord Carrington told him that if our proposals were not accepted the patient would die anyway. General Walls had been brought to accept them on condition that there would be no interference with the security forces and that, in the final phase of the negotiations, we would not make proposals for the cease-fire which were unacceptable to the Rhodesian military com-manders. But for these assurances, there was no chance of getting the Mu-zorewa Government to agree to surrender power—and it was perhaps the most remarkable development of the Conference that they were brought to do so. In a final very tense meeting with the Salisbury delegation, on 25 October, when accused by Mr Smith of dragging out the Conference while people were being killed in Rhodesia Lord Carrington reacted with under-standable indignation in an exchange which revealed the extent to which Mr Smith was now isolated. The Salisbury delegation accepted our pro-posals and their agreement to stand aside placed the Patriotic Front in a difficult position. As they continued to argue for a UN force etc., Lord Carrington said that we were not prepared to accept elements falling out-side the Lusaka agreement. It would be for us to supervise the elections; there was no question of UN involvement.

40. We had to face the possibility that the Patriotic Front would not agree to the transitional arrangements while Bishop Muzorewa had agreed to the constitution, new elections and a British Governor with executive authority. This was a prospect most of our friends and allies were ex-tremely reluctant to face. But it would have been fatal to the chances of getting the Salisbury delegation to accept the Governor's authority and of a wider agreement if the Patriotic Front had been allowed to exercise a veto. It was clear that there would be applause so long as we remained on the tightrope and a fairly general rush for cover as soon as we fell off.

41. This presented the Government with a serious dilemma. In one sense the least risky course if we failed to achieve a wider agreement was to grant legal independence to Rhodesia forthwith on the basis of a new constitution. But this would attract little international support; nor would a return to legality with the Muzorewa Government in place. To assume

direct responsibility for Rhodesia while the war continued clearly carried enormous risks. Yet it was necessary to face those risks if we were to create a situation in which the pressures on the Patriotic Front to participate would be maximised and the chances of weakening international support for them would be greatest if they refused to do so.

42. Informal contacts with Mr Nkomo had been maintained throughout the Conference. At this stage we began a series of private meetings with him and Mr Chambati. In the early stages these were devoted to a further attempt to convince Mr Nkomo that the British Government wanted to see a settlement in which he could participate; and that if he did so, we would see to it that he had a fair chance in elections. It was emphasised that this really was the last chance and that the alternative was a fight to the finish. Mr Nkomo was concerned about the consequences of failure and conscious that this was unlikely to turn to his political benefit. It seemed clear that he would prefer a settlement if we could make it possible for him to drag his ZANU allies in. But there were the usual indications of chronic indecision, a desire to have the best of both worlds and a real fear of any action which might lead him to be accused of splitting the Patriotic Front.

43. As the 15 November deadline approached it was clear that any attempt to renew Section 2 of the Southern Rhodesia Act, even for the limited period necessary to bring the Conference to a conclusion, would place the Government in difficulties with its own supporters. This would, furthermore, have been regarded as a breach of faith by the Salisbury delegation. For some time, therefore, we had been considering ways of seeking to turn the parliamentary deadline to advantage in the negotiations. It was in any event desirable to replace the general enabling powers which would lapse with Section 2; and to expand these to enable us to make provisions for the independence constitution and new elections. The introduction of an enabling Bill at this stage was designed to increase the momentum towards a settlement by:

(*a*) giving the Government all the powers it needed to make provision for the independence constitution, new elections and a return to legality;

(*b*) thereby demonstrating to both sides that we meant business and intended to proceed with a settlement;

(*c*) reassuring the Salisbury delegation who by this stage were threatening to withdraw from the Conference in protest at the apparent ability of the Patriotic Front to drag it out indefinitely;

(*d*) bringing home to the Patriotic Front that if they did not agree to the pre-independence arrangements they would not be permitted to block the process leading to independence.

At the same time it was made clear to Bishop Muzorewa's delegation that the removal of the generality of the sanctions would take place on the day the Governor arrived in Salisbury and not before.

44. President Kaunda was invited to London as the moment of decision on the pre-independence arrangement approached. He had more to gain than almost anyone from the success of the negotiations. But in discussion of the problem he tended to be both vague and emotional and rarely seemed prepared to bring home to the Patriotic Front the need to take account of Zambian interests. The difficulties of communication were compounded by the personality of his special adviser, Mr Mark Chona, who was in London through most of the Conference. Mr Chona showed an ambition parallel only to that of President Nyerere to dictate the terms of a settlement, down to the smallest detail. Tortuous and suspicious, he frequently seemed to be more intransigent than the Patriotic Front and his advice to President Kaunda, as reflected in messages from the President, at times showed him to be defending positions already abandoned by Mr Nkomo.

45. The Prime Minister and Lord Carrington told President Kaunda that there was a serious risk of the Salisbury delegation leaving the Conference if we allowed the Patriotic Front to continue to filibuster. President Kaunda was given a paper which lifted the veil on our proposals for the cease-fire, including the establishment of a cease-fire commission and a monitoring force, as well as an assurance that arrangements would be made for the Patriotic Front forces. The Prime Minister told him that the key to peace was in his hands. We were doing all we could to give effect to the Lusaka agreement. An agreement was attainable on this but not on some other basis. Unlike previous attempts to achieve a settlement, we were in a positon to put these plans into effect. Mr Nkomo was showing more interest in an agreement than Mr Mugabe. It would be a tragedy if the chance was lost.

46. President Kaunda reacted positively, Mr Nkomo, who was aware that there would be a return to legality whether or not the Patriotic Front agreed, realised that a decision could no longer be delayed. In private meetings, he abandoned his arguments for a governing council etc. But he had to carry his own military commanders with him and to save face. His main concern was with the status of the Patriotic Front forces. But Mr Mugabe was still far from agreeing and President Nyerere was intensifying his efforts to persuade all and sundry of the unreasonableness of our proposals. The difficulty in relation to the forces was the acute sensitivity of the Salisbury delegation to any suggestion of 'equality of status'. We agreed with Mr Nkomo the simple addition to our paper: 'The Patriotic Front's forces will also be required to comply with the directions of the Governor'. The Salisbury delegation could hardly refuse to accept this. On

14 November in a critical phase of the Conference, Lord Carrington told the Patriotic Front leaders that if it was not possible to reach agreement, he would have to report the position to his Cabinet colleagues at 10.30 a.m. on the next day and ask them to decide our future course of action. On the following morning, in a private meeting with Lord Carrington, it was clear that Mr Nkomo was prepared to agree. Mr Mugabe was much more reluctant. The Patriotic Front leaders were aware by this time that the enabling Bill had passed both Houses of Parliament and that, if they refused, it was open to the Government to begin to proceed with the internal parties. After a break during which the Patriotic Front leaders conferred together, a plenary session was held at 10 a.m. Mr Mugabe stated that with the addition to our paper they could accept the interim proposals, subject to a successful outcome of the negotiations on the cease-fire.

47. Each successive phase of the Conference was more difficult than the last. The problem which caused us most difficulty, as we had always known it would, was that of the military arrangements for the cease-fire and the separation of the forces. Hence the strategy of tackling the military problems only after agreement on the political issues had created an expectation of success. It was necessary to carry the Rhodesian commanders with us, failing which there would be no settlement to implement. Bishop Muzorewa was in no position to overrule them. The opposing forces were inextricably entangled throughout Rhodesia. The Rhodesians would not agree to a cease-fire *sur place*. This would in any case have been certain to break down and would have rendered impossible any effective monitoring arrangement. They wanted the Patriotic Front's forces to withdraw across the frontiers; or, failing that, no cease-fire at all. They were haunted by the dangers of 'relinquishing control'. They argued that any arrangements which gave the Patriotic Front forces a recognised status within Rhodesia would be damaging to Bishop Muzorewa and virtually impossible to control militarily. They did not believe that there would be a fully effective cease-fire and in this they were quite right. We too felt that it was sensible to plan on the basis of a partially effective cease-fire. General Walls made it clear at every stage that any requirement that the Rhodesian forces must cease patrolling would result in the withdrawal of his support for a settlement. He had agreed to the appointment of a British Governor only on the understanding that command and control of the armed forces remained in his hands.

48. The problem of the separation of the forces was bound to be the most difficult aspect of the cease-fire negotiations. We therefore decided to leave this to the last and to seek agreement first to the other elements, including the cease-fire commission. No previous British Government had envisaged sending British troops to Rhodesia; and there were obvious risks

in doing so. Yet it was clear that no cease-fire could be maintained without a monitoring force. General Walls was brought to agree to a force under British auspices with limited participation from Commonwealth countries not committed to support for the Patriotic Front (Australia, New Zealand, Fiji and Kenya). The Government concluded that a readiness to take responsibility for the monitoring force and to make by far the major contribution to it was essential to a serious attempt to reach a settlement.

49. It was clear that the demarcation of zones between the two sides would have been impossible to negotiate. The Patriotic Front forces would have to assemble and be identified if their activities were to be monitored and their security guaranteed. This was made clear to President Kaunda and to Mr Nkomo before the Patriotic Front agreed to the interim arrangements. The Rhodesians also demanded the monitoring of Patriotic Front bases outside Rhodesia.

50. Our problems were increased by the Rhodesian refusal to engage in direct negotiations with the Patriotic Front commanders, just as the Patriotic Front had refused to negotiate with Bishop Muzorewa. Tongogara insisted that he should deal with General Walls. We needed no convincing of this but found that, as in the previous phases of the Conference, we had no option but to undertake ourselves the negotiations with both sides. In the earlier stages of the Conference it had become clear that Tongogara was interested in a settlement. Indeed his turned out to be the strongest voice in ZANU in favour of one. In the cease-fire negotiations he established a good relationship with General Farndale and the rest of the British team: there was apparent in his attitude the hankering of a successful guerrilla leader after recognition. The Rhodesians insisted that the assembly process must be completed within seven days: they could not afford to relinquish control for longer. While his political leaders were still arguing that the cease-fire would take two months to bring into effect, Tongogara did not pretend that he could not get orders through to all his forces within a few days.

51. At this stage the prospects of success in the Conference were very nearly upset by massive Rhodesian raids into Zambia in response to large scale infiltration by ZIPRA. Mr Nkomo was trying desperately to get as many men as possible into Rhodesia in anticipation either of a settlement or of the need to try to intensify the war if we were proceeding without him. The raids were ordered by the military commanders in Salisbury without reference to General Walls. They did impede ZIPRA movement towards the Rhodesian border. But they were also clearly designed to damage the Zambian infrastructure. President Kaunda professed to be convinced that the attacks had been authorised by us. Demonstrations were

organised outside the High Commission in Lusaka and Sir Leonard Allinson had to be withdrawn. The Rhodesians were warned of the consequences of any further raids, except on guerrilla targets in close proximity to the frontier. We were able just in time to prevent them blowing up the Tete suspension bridge in Mozambique.

52. As the military temperature continued to rise we concluded that if the Patriotic Front could be brought to accept our general cease-fire proposals we must devise a plan to deal with the danger of indefinitely prolonged discussions of the arrangements for their implementation. We should also take advantage of the favourable circumstances which would then have been created to effect the return to legality in conditions in which we could hope to secure a good deal of acquiescence. There would be protests from the Patriotic Front but there would then cease from their point of view to be any advantage in further delay. To make the final arrangements for the cease-fire we needed a presence in Salisbury.

53. In private discussion Mr Nkomo was still saying that he could not accept the cease-fire proposals. Our assessment was that he did intend to accept eventually. The Salisbury delegation were by this time in a state of extreme agitation, as they considered that they were losing ground militarily. To step up the pressure on the Patriotic Front, on 3 December the Government made the Order in Council making provision for a Governor. Lord Carrington gave a press conference stating that we were beginning to take the Legislative action to put the settlement into effect, but in such a way as to leave it open for the Patriotic Front to participate. By this stage we had reached virtual agreement with Mr Nkomo. Lord Carrington told the Patriotic Front that we would not carry out a purge of the forces on either side; but there would be no external intervention in Rhodesia under a British Governor. The Patriotic Front agreed to the cease-fire subject to the details of implementation.

54. The argument now turned on the dispositions of the forces. The Rhodesian commanders had with difficulty been brought to agree to the allocation of fifteen assembly places for the Patriotic Front forces inside Rhodesia and thirty rendezvous positions to enable them to get there. Most of the assembly places were in peripheral areas which had long been subject to guerrilla activity and in which the Rhodesians exercised only intermittent control. Fortunately these dispositions corresponded to Tongogara's concern that his forces should not be 'encircled' and that there should be an easy escape route into Mozambique. But both he and, on political grounds, Mr Nkomo were very concerned about the absence of an assembly area in the Midlands. At no stage did we indicate that the Rhodesian forces would be confined to barracks and, if we had done so, this would have been a breaking point with the Rhodesian delegation. We

based our doctrine on reciprocal disengagement. The disposition of the Rhodesian forces would depend on the assembly process. If, after the end of the assembly process, forces were found in the field with their weapons they would have to be dealt with by the forces which had accepted the Governor's authority. This was clearly stipulated in the cease-fire agreement and the military talks with Tongogara. There was no doubt in his mind what was meant—though the Patriotic Front argued then as later that their forces should play a role in policing the cease-fire.

55. The Patriotic Front had only been pushed over the previous hurdles by the threat of proceeding without them. On this occasion they were being asked to take the final decision which committed them to the whole agreement. Their tactics throughout the Conference had been to avoid saying 'yes' or 'no'. We did not believe that they could be brought to the point of final decision unless we actually effected the return to legality. Otherwise they would have every incentive to continue to drag out the Conference while infiltrating the remainder of their forces into Rhodesia to which the Rhodesians would have responded with further attacks on Zambia and Mozambique. The Prime Minister had decided that, in the event of a comprehensive settlement, the Governor should be Lord Soames. The choice of a senior Cabinet Minister was intended to demonstrate the Government's determination to carry the settlement through. Clearly, however, there were risks in sending a Cabinet Minister to Salisbury with the war continuing. In that event, it was thought, it might be more appropriate to send a 'professional' Governor. As it became clear that unless we moved quickly to effect the return to legality the chance of a settlement was liable to be lost as a result of a military crisis or the withdrawal of the Salisbury delegation, the Government had to decide whether to risk sending Lord Soames. His appointment was announced on 7 December as was the intention that he should arrive in Salisbury in the following week.

56. The cease-fire proposals were completed with the distribution of a map setting out the Patriotic Front assembly places and the monitoring arrangements for the Rhodesian forces. The return to legality was affected by the arrival of the Governor in Salisbury and the acceptance of his authority on 12 December. The Salisbury Parliament had been dissolved. Sir Anthony Parsons informed the Security Council of the return to legality and that sanctions were being lifted immediately. The chances of finally pushing the Patriotic Front into a settlement depended in part on the extent of the international support we received. Otherwise they would be encouraged to hold out and make further demands which would not be negotiable.

57. The decision to send the Governor, although essential to bring the Conference to a conclusion, caused heart-searching among our allies who

remained reluctant to be confronted with anything approaching a choice between us and the Patriotic Front. There were divided views in the US Administration: Ambassador McHenry had been arguing that the Americans must 'save the British from themselves'. It required a personal message from the Prime Minister to President Carter to push the Americans over the hurdle of lifting sanctions on 16 December, a move which helped to bring home the Patriotic Front the consequences of failing to participate in the settlement.

58. Mr Nkomo was by this time ready to agree on condition he secured one additional assembly place. The Conference actually ended on 15 December, however, with Mr Mugabe launching a bitter attack on our proposals and making ready to leave for New York to address the United Nations. We had kept in close touch with President Machel and in daily touch with his special adviser, Mr Fernando Honwana, who alone of the frontline representatives played a crucial role in the negotiations. President Machel told Mr Mugabe that if he did not participate in the settlement he should not count on continued Mozambican support. General Tongogara, after hesitating about the military arrangements, also came down in favour of agreement. On 17 December Mr Nkomo and Mr Mugabe initialled the agreement.

59. The final phase had run us into the most serious difficulties with the Rhodesians. The Rhodesian military commanders had with extreme reluctance been persuaded to agree to one additional assembly place to bring in Mr Nkomo. The discovery that ZANU were going to participate in the settlement as well very nearly led to the withdrawal of their support for it. They pushed Bishop Muzorewa into insisting on 'clarifications'. Above all they demanded a firm undertaking that the Governor would take action against any party which systematically broke the cease-fire or practised intimidation on a massive scale. This undertaking and its interpretation were to be the subject of a running battle with the Rhodesian commanders throughout the Governor's administration.

60. The successful completion of what appeared at the outset an almost impossible negotiation was attributable to a number of factors. The frontline countries were looking for an escape from the war; the Lusaka agreement offered them one. The Rhodesians knew that they could no longer carry on without an agreement with us. Mr Smith was not able to bring his negative influence so directly to bear. Mr Nkomo was conscious that this was his last chance, but frightened of being accused of splitting the Patriotic Front. Despite subsequent difficulties with him, General Walls' influence in favour of a settlement was crucial. The South Africans were persuaded to acquiesce. We found an unexpected ally in President Machel, who put more pressure on the Patriotic Front to agree than any of the other

front-line Presidents.

61. The time was right. This would not, however, have been of much avail without the determination with which the Government tackled the problem and the manner in which the Secretary of State conducted the negotiations. It was the ambition of everyone involved in them finally to discharge our responsibility to bring Rhodesia to legal independence; and to do so in a fashion which would enhance our reputation and not diminish it. The Government took the difficult and courageous decisions to send the Governor to Rhodesia in advance of final agreement in the Conference; and to send several hundred British troops to monitor a precarious cease-fire. Without a willingness to take those decisions and face the risks they involved, a settlement would not have been achieved. There remained the fundamental difficulty that the Rhodesians were never really reconciled to the participation of ZANU. It had been clear at every stage of the negotiations that, if a comprehensive agreement could be negotiated, it would be no less difficult to put it into effect.

11 July 1980   R.W. RENWICK

THE RHODESIA SETTLEMENT

1. Introduction

1. The negotiating tactics adopted at Lancaster House were based on a study of the Kissinger initiative, the breakdown of the Geneva Conference and the subsequent failure of negotiations on the Anglo-American proposals.

2. By 1976 the situation for which the six principles (Annex A) had originally been designed—the granting of independence in advance of but with guarantees of unimpeded progress to majority rule—had long since been overtaken. The Pearce Commission had concluded that the last serious attempt to reach a settlement on that basis was not acceptable to the people of Rhodesia. The granting of independence to Mozambique, the closure of the border and the support given by the FRELIMO Government to the ZANLA (Mugabe) forces operating from its territory transformed the time-scale for Rhodesia's prospects of survival.

3. The South African Government, conscious of the dangers of being drawn into increasingly direct support for a regime in Rhodesia which no longer had any long term prospects of survival—and of Mr Smith's attempts to appeal over their heads to South African opinion—began at last actively seeking to promote a political settlement and had shown that they were prepared to put pressure on Mr Smith. By 1976 they had concluded that the best course was to work for the emergence of a moderate black Government. In June 1976 a meeting with Mr Vorster convinced Dr Kissinger that if the British and American Governments could produce a viable plan for a settlement, the South Africans would help to 'deliver' Mr Smith. There were consultations between the British and American Governments about proposals for the transition leading to independence (though the idea of a British Governor was rejected at this time by the Government, who saw dangers in Britain getting too directly involved). On 19 September Dr Kissinger persuaded Mr Smith to accept five points drafted by the Americans. Dr Kissinger gave Mr Smith the impression that he had obtained the agreement of Presidents Kaunda and Nyerere to the five points. Mr Smith announced his acceptance of them in Salisbury on 24 September.

4. Mr Smith emphasized that what he had agreed with Dr Kissinger constituted a package deal including the lifting of sanctions and an injection of development capital. The five points provided for majority rule within two years. The Rhodesian Government would meet with African leaders to organise an interim Government until majority rule was

achieved. This would consist of a Council of State, half of whose members would be black and half white, with a white chairman without a special vote; and a Council of Ministers with a majority of Africans and an African First Minister. The Ministers of Defence and Law and Order would be white. Decisions of the Council of Ministers would be taken by a two-thirds majority. On the establishment of the interim Government, sanctions would be lifted and all acts of war, including guerrilla warfare, would cease.

5. The five points were drafted in such categoric fashion that Mr Smith could and did take them as a firm agreement. They appeared to lay down clearly the form the interim Government was to take. Control over the armed forces and police would be in white hands during the transition. The white representatives would have a veto over decisions of the Council of State and the Council of Ministers. Since these bodies would have the task of working out the majority rule constitution, there was no guarantee of early progress in doing so. But sanctions would have been lifted and, it was hoped, the war halted from the beginning of the process. The front line Presidents had not in fact agreed to these arrangements and they had never been discussed with the external nationalist leaders. Dr Kissinger had cut his corners in this respect. The inclusion of the provision that the Minister of Defence and Law and Order must be white had been Mr Smith's price for his acceptance of the 'package'. But, with South African help, Dr Kissinger had extracted for the first time from Mr Smith acceptance of majority rule.

6. The Geneva Conference probably never had a chance of success. The 'package' was not accepted by the front line Presidents or the external leaders. There was no agreed basis for negotiations. Mr Smith claimed that its sole purpose was to choose member for the Council State, which would be the supreme constitutional authority during the interim period. On the eve of the conference, under pressure from the front line Presidents, Mr Nkomo and Mr Mugabe agreed to negotiate together as joint leaders of the Patriotic Front. In all other respects ZANU and ZAPU remained separate entities. The early days were spent in procedural wrangles, with the Patriotic Front objecting that the conference should have been chaired by a British Cabinet Minister and demanding more generous accommodation allowances. With wide differences over the fundamental question of who was to exercise power during the interim, and with whose forces, the British delegation were reduced to trying to get agreement on the date for the achievement of majority rule. Within a few days it was apparent that there was no prospect of agreement to the Kissinger proposals. Mr Mugabe did not appear to believe in the possibility of a negotiated solution. The con-

ference dragged on until December, achieving nothing. The final break-down came because of Mr Smith's refusal to negotiate on anything except the package he had agreed with Dr Kissinger. With the change of administration in the United States Dr Kissinger himself was unable to do anything to help retrieve the situation.

7. By this stage the British Government had agreed that plans for the interim might include the participation of a British Commissioner with certain limited functions. Mr Smith rejected this proposal: the idea of surrendering power to a British representative was anathema to him. Bishop Muzorewa, finding himself rejected by the front line Presidents, was tempted to make his own agreement with Mr Smith. Mr Smith broke off the Geneva Conference and subsequent contacts because he thought he perceived a respectable escape route from the prospect of uncontrolled majority rule. He calculated that if he could get Bishop Muzorewa on his side he would be able to establish a form of Government with African support while leaving him and his followers in a position of considerable influence; and that while the Rhodesian security forces could not contain the guerrillas indefinitely, they could do so for long enough to enable him to work out an agreement with the internal parties. The South Africans were attracted by a solution of this kind.

8. At the end of 1978 the prospects for a negotiated settlement could hardly have looked less promising. The Anglo/American proposals put forward by Dr Owen and Mr Vance of 1 September 1977 had run into fundamental objections from the Patriotic Front and the internal parties. Those proposals envisaged the surrender of power by the Rhodesian regime; the return of Rhodesia to the legal status of a British dependent territory; the establishment by the British Government of a transitional administration under a British Commissioner with the task of conducting elections within six months to decide the independence Government; a United Nations presence, including a UN force; and a democratic independence constitution. The future Zimbabwe national army would be 'based on the liberation forces'. This last proviso deprived the Anglo-American proposals from the outset of any possibility of being accepted by the Salisbury administration and therefore of ever being implemented. President Carter was talked into a commitment to this effect by President Nyerere.

9. When these proposals were discussed with them in Malta between 30 January and 1 February 1978 and, subsequently, in Dar es Salaam in April, Mr Nkomo and Mr Mugabe insisted that the Patriotic Front must superintend the transitional process. Their counter-proposals for the transition envisaged a governing council which should consist of a British

Commissioner, a representative of the settler community and four members of the Patriotic Front. The Patriotic Front must have a 'dominant role in the sovereign body'. The regime's forces must be demobilised. They resisted any role for the internal parties and indeed the whole idea that there were other parties to the negotiation. It was up to the British and American Governments to deliver Mr Smith.

10. This they were not in a position to do. The Rhodesian authorities were not ready to surrender power or to accept a British Commissioner with 'dictatorial' powers. Nor were they prepared to accept a United Nations force. They regarded the proposition that the future army should be based on the liberation forces as in any event pre-judging that entire outcome in favour of the Patriotic Front. Mr Smith and his colleagues proceeded instead with the agreement with the internal parties signed in Salisbury 3 March 1978. That agreement included constitutional arrangements providing for majority rule based on universal adult suffrage; a 100 member legislative assembly with 72 black and 28 white seats; a declaration of rights and provision for the independence of the judiciary and the public services; and the establishment of a transitional Government with an Executive Council consisting of Mr Smith, Bishop Muzorewa, the Rev Sithole and Chief Chirau. The aim was to achieve independence on the basis of majority rule by 31 December 1978.

11. In August Mr Smith held a secret meeting with Mr Nkomo in Lusaka at which he offered him a leading place in the transitional administration. The meeting was encouraged by President Kaunda and the Nigerian Government. President Nyerere and Mr Mugabe were highly suspicious and, as soon as he found out about it, President Nyerere leaked news of the meeting. The possibility of further direct talks between Mr Smith and Mr Nkomo was destroyed by the reactions to the shooting down by ZIPRA of an Air Rhodesia Viscount at Kariba on 3 September.

12. At the end of the year Lord Cledwyn-Hughes concluded that an all-party conference would have no chance of success. The Patriotic Front believed that it could achieve its aims by continuing the war. The Salisbury parties would be prepared only to offer the Patriotic Front a place within the internal settlement. If the security situation worsened, as it probably would, the Salisbury parties might become less determined on their present course of action—but this in turn would lead the Patriotic Front to strengthen its demands.

13. The Rhodesians pressed ahead with the internal settlement. On 30 January 1979, out of a total European electorate of 94,700 57,269 voted in favour of the new constitution—representing a 'yes' vote of 85 per cent in a poll of 71.5 per cent.

Annex A

The Six Principles

In 1965 the British Government listed five principles on which it would
need to be satisfied before contemplating independence for Rhodesia:

1. The principle and intention of majority rule, already enshrined in the
   1961 constitution, would have to be maintained and guaranteed;
2. There would have to be guarantees against retrogressive amendment
   of the constitution;
3. There would have to be immediate improvement in the political status of the African population;
4. There would have to be progress towards ending racial discrimina-
   tion;
5. The British Government would need to be satisfied that any basis for
   independence was acceptable to the people of Rhodesia as a whole.

A sixth principle was added in 1966:

6. It would be necessary to ensure that, regardless of race, there was no
   oppression of majority by minority or of minority by majority

2. The Options (May 1979)

1. Although Rhodesia did not figure in the election campaign it was
generally regarded as the foreign policy issue on which the Conservative
and Labour parties were furthest apart. The Conservatives had strongly
criticised the Labour Government's handling of the problem and failure to
give encouragement to the internal settlement. The Conservative Party
manifesto stated that: 'the Conservative Party will aim to achieve a lasting
settlement to the Rhodesia problem based on the democratic wishes of the
people of that country. If the six principles which all British Governments
have supported for the last fifteen years are fully satisfied following the
present Rhodesian election, the next Government will have the duty to return Rhodesia to a state of legality, move to lift sanctions and to do its
utmost to ensure that a new independent state gains international recognition'. The Leader of the Opposition sent a team of observers led by Lord
Boyd to witness the Rhodesian elections. It was made quite clear that the
policy of a Conservative Government would be strongly influenced by his
report.

2. On 24 April the results of the Rhodesian elections were announced.
Bishop Muzorewa's party, the UANC, won 1.2 million votes, over two-
thirds of the votes cast, and 51 seats. The Reverend Sithole, disappointed
at his failure to win more than 12 seats, denounced the results as a fraud.
Chief Ndiweni's regional party won 9 seats in Matabeleland. As a result

of the massive call-up of white reservists over the election period, the Patriotic Front proved unable to disrupt the elections or to prevent a high turn-out. Nearly two-thirds of the electorate voted.

3. On 4 May the Department submitted to the incoming Secretary of State a paper discussing future policy options and their implications. Recalling the six principles and the obligations imposed on us by mandatory resolutions of the UN Security Council, this stated that a Parliament had now been elected in Rhodesia on the basis of universal adult suffrage, but in circumstances which were unlikely to satisfy international opinion generally as to the significance of the result. The country was under majority rule in the sense that the future Prime Minister, a majority of the Government and the majority of Parliament would be African. The Constitution had been endorsed by a referendum of the white electorate, but not submitted to any test of acceptability by the African population. It represented a major advance, but guaranteed the whites representation greatly out of proportion to their numbers in both Government and Parliament, and effectively removed a large measure of control over the public services, the security forces and the judiciary from the executive for the next ten years. These and other provisions had been criticised as contradicting claims that Rhodesia had achieved genuine majority rule.

4. The Patriotic Front would continue the war. They had the support of the great majority of African states, who would demand the continuance of sanctions and the withholding of recognition. Victory was not in sight for either side. The neighbouring countries were increasingly affected by the conflict and there was a serious risk of increased Soviet and other Communist involvement on the side of the Patriotic Front (for whom they were already providing arms, equipment, training and political indoctrination) and of increased Soviet involvement in the neighbouring states. The security situation had deteriorated steadily over the last three years. The front line states—Zambia, Tanzania, Botswana, Mozambique and Angola—had reasons for self-interest to want a settlement. But they did not regard themselves as able to accept one which excluded the Patriotic Front. There was no prospect of an early change in this attitude. The South African objective was to avoid the emergence of Government dominated by the Patriotic Front. They would support a Muzorewa-led Government so long as they believed it had significant prospects of survival. They would, however, continue to be wary of committing combat troops and to linking their fate too closely with that of the Rhodesian administration if the security situation continued to deteriorate.

5. The aim of successive British Governments had been to grant legal independence to Rhodesia on terms which would be internationally acceptable, enable sanctions to be lifted and end the war. That aim might not

be attainable in full. All attempts to promote an all-party settlement with an agreed constitution and elections under international supervision had failed. The new situation inside the country, however, might offer some opportunities to approximate to that overall objective. The Government would be under strong pressure to make some gesture of support to the new administration in Salisbury.

6. Against this background, papers were submitted discussing four broad alternative approaches:

Option A was to invite Parliament to declare that Rhodesia was no longer part of Her Majesty's dominions and that we no longer had responsibility or jurisdiction for it. This would involve the repeal of the Southern Rhodesia Act 1965 and the dismantling of sanctions. We would not get Security Council endorsement for our legal argument that with the granting of legal independence sanctions should fall away. It would be argued that a threat to the peace continued to exist. Such action was unlikely to command the support of the US administration or of most members of the Nine. We could expect strong reactions in Africa and the Commonwealth, not confined to the more radical members. Nigeria and Zambia among others would be likely to break off diplomatic relations and take action against our economic interests. British communities and interests in other African countries would be at risk. There would be a high risk of increased Soviet/Cuban involvement in the war. We would quickly be confronted by requests from Salisbury for arms supplies. We could find ourselves in a very exposed position in support of the Rhodesian regime in the company of South Africa in opposition to virtually all African and Commonwealth opinion.

Option B assumed that the Government might choose not to seek parliamentary approval in November for the renewal of Section 2 of the Southern Rhodesia Act 1965. If Congress obliged the US Administration to lift sanctions the positions in Britain and the United States would be similar. But our legal argument concerning sanctions was that the determination under Chapter VII of the UN Charter that a threat to the peace existed in Rhodesia was based on the existence of a state of rebellion in that territory. (Apart from its juridical merits, this doctrine was the means by which successive British Governments had sought to ensure that the ultimate responsibility to decide what happened in relation to Rhodesia rested with the British Parliament and not with the Security Council.) A failure to maintain sanctions without a return to legality would put the Government in breach of its treaty obligations under Article 25 of the UN Charter.

Option C was to seek improvements to the Constitution and the way in which it was operated including censorship, executions under martial law, etc. HMG might offer to conduct a test of the acceptability of an 'improved' settlement. We could aim for Mr Smith to be obliged to make a definitive exit from politics and for the Patriotic Front to be offered terms for their return to political life which could put them in difficulty if they refused. But even an 'improved' internal settlement would be unlikely to attract the participation of the Patriotic Front or the support of the front line Presidents. The war would continue.

Option D was to make a fresh attempt to end the war. It would be put to Bishop Muzorewa that the Government recognised the extent of the progress which had been made, but the central problem remained the war. It was not realistic for him to think that HMG could itself end it or ensure general recognition of his Government. It was still incumbent on us to make an effort to achieve a settlement. It would be in the Bishop's interest to cooperate in an effort to mount a negotiation involving all the parties. If this approach did not achieve its primary objective because the Patriotic Front adopted an intransigent attitude, we might be in a stronger position to exercise one of the other options. It would allow time for consultation with the parties and governments concerned and with Bishop Muzorewa.

7. The paper pointed out that these approaches were not mutually exclusive. There would be much to be said for demonstrating from the outset a sympathetic attitude to the Bishop and his Government, not least so as to be in a position to influence them; we should establish a senior official in Salisbury. The international dimensions which the Rhodesia problem had acquired were such that any approach to it by HMG must, to have any prospect of success, be based on careful consultation with the United States, our European partners and the African Commonwealth. Such a process could be initiated by a mission led by a senior political figure to the other African capitals particularly concerned.

8. The Department also provided an analysis of the *Rhodesian elections*, in advance of Lord Boyd's report. The turnout of 64.45 per cent was impressive, as was the conduct of the ballot. Despite the Reverend Sithole's allegations of irregularities, the general view was that the elections had been fairly conducted in terms of a competition between the parties participating in them. The constitutional arrangements had not been voted on by the African population. It was therefore much more difficult to judge whether they were 'acceptable to the people of Rhodesia as a whole'; and whether the elections were 'free and fair' in terms of giving the African population a free choice as to their future political leaders. There had been strong pressure on the African population to vote. It would be argued that elections held under censorship and martial law and with the external parties banned could not be regarded as representing the wishes of the people of Rhodesia as a whole. Formally the external parties had been invited to

participate, but under the existing administration and security forces—an arrangement it was known they would not accept. The elections had exposed the emptiness of the Patriotic Front's military claims; but ZANU in particular could be expected to go on fighting with a new determination.

9. An analysis of *the Constitution* noted that the white minority, with twenty-eight of the one hundred seats in the House of Assembly, were in a position to block the amendment of all entrenched provisions of the Constitution (124 sections out of 170, including all the politically sensitive provisions) and a wide range of existing legislation. Amendment in these areas could only be carried with the support of seventy-eight members of the House of Assembly. The white members were also entitled to between one fourth and one third of all Cabinet seats. The arrangements concerning the judiciary indicated a determination to keep the High Court in European hands for many years to come. In the making of appointments to key posts in the public service, the effective power lay exclusively with the Public Service Commission. These provisions threw doubt on the extent to which there would be a real transfer of power in the administration and to which it would be possible to pursue an effective policy of Africanisation. The provisions relating to the police force and the defence force were designed to withhold effective control over those forces from Ministers and Parliament and to keep it in European hands. The Commanders of those forces were not appointed by the Government and could not be removed by it.

10. A study of the *security situation* noted the steady worsening of the position since 1976. At that time the country was still relatively calm and the possibility that a guerrilla war could induce the regime to concede the principle of black majority rule within two years seemed remote. The nationalist leaders were divided and no more than three to four hundred guerrillas were present inside the country. The steady build-up of guerrilla operations from the second half of 1976 was not halted by the high 'kill ratio' achieved by the security forces. As early as August 1976 a confidential assessment circulated to members of the Rhodesian Cabinet concluded that guerrilla recruitment continued to rise while the limits of white manpower were being approached; and that Rhodesia would be overwhelmed by internal and external pressures unless a settlement was concluded. The burden of national service and the frequency of call-up of the white reservists had increased dramatically. The small but efficient air force had very limited resources. The only areas not yet substantially affected by the war were Salisbury and Bulawayo. Communications had been severely curtailed. Cross-border raids had inflicted considerable casualties on the guerrillas. But the death toll in 1978, at nearly 5,500, was equal to the two previous years combined. The casualty rate in 1979 was likely to be twice that of 1978. Since 1976 net European emigration had run at a consistently

high level—approximately 14,000 whites were estimated to have left in 1978, over 2,700 in December alone. The burden of defence expenditure was heavy; there had been a decline since 1976 in industrial production; and employment was not expanding at a rate sufficient to absorb African school-leavers. The Patriotic Front had no capacity to confront the Rhodesian security forces, but believed that they could win a war of attrition. The tide had been running slowly in their favour. In the short term the war was likely to continue on its present course, with the Rhodesians using pre-emptive strikes as a primary means of defence; with guerrilla attacks on soft targets and the guerrillas, especially ZANLA, gradually extending their influence over the Tribal Trust Lands. The morale of the white community was crucial and would be affected by any outbreak of urban terrorism.

11. A note on *British interests* in Africa drew attention to the importance of our exports to Nigeria (£1133 million in 1978).

12. In view of the general belief that *United Kingdom sanctions* against Rhodesia depended entirely on Section 2 of the Southern Rhodesia Act 1965, which fell to be renewed annually in November, a final paper explained that a considerable body of sanctions derived from legislation which did not depend on Section 2 and would remain in force unless the Government took positive steps to repeal it. There could be no question of going against the will of Parliament in relation to the lifting of sanctions— or of the Government relying on the votes of the opposition to secure their continuance. This note was, however, intended to indicate that the Government's freedom of manoeuvre—and its ability, if necessary, to put pressure on the Salisbury parties—was somewhat greater than at the time was generally supposed.

3. The First Steps (May-June 1979)

1. After discussions with officials based on these papers Lord Carrington formed his views on the best way to proceed. It was already clear that Mr Ian Smith's insistence on remaining in the Government after the elections, despite repeated promises to withdraw, would further reduce the prospects of recognition by any other African state. On 11 May Lord Carrington circulated a memorandum (OD(79)3) to his ministerial colleagues in the Defence and Overseas Policy Committee of the Cabinet. This stated that the Government's objectives were to bring Rhodesia back to legality and to do its utmost to ensure that Rhodesia gained widespread international recognition. Lord Boyd seemed likely to conclude that the election in Rhodesia had been fairly conducted and as free as was possible in the circumstances. It was open to the Government to grant legal independence

to Rhodesia and to lift sanctions. This would be widely popular in the Conservative party and in the country; but we could be of more assistance to Rhodesia by proceeding differently. To recognise immediately would risk considerable damage to British interests, both economic and political, throughout the world. The aim must be to return Rhodesia to legality in such a way and on such a time-scale that the country was launched into independence with the best start that was attainable, while at the same time limiting damage to British interests.

2. Immediate recognition would not bring the war to an end, nor achieve international acceptance. Few if any of our allies and partners would follow suit. It would be likely to harden attitudes in Africa, the Commonwealth and the third world. There was a need for consultations with friendly countries, starting with the Americans.

3. In view of the change of circumstances inside Rhodesia it was not possible to envisage asking Parliament in November to renew Section 2 of the 1965 Act. Although this would not remove all sanctions, it would put us in breach of our obligations under mandatory Security Council Resolutions if we had not by then secured a return to legality. Our objective should be to ensure that sanctions were lifted not only by us but by other members of the international community.

4. The first task must be to put ourselves in a position to influence the new Rhodesian Government. Lord Carrington had already arranged for Sir Antony Duff to visit Salisbury for discussions with Bishop Muzorewa. The Government should appoint a senior figure to advise on the steps to be taken to bring Rhodesia to a state of legality and international recognition, involving consultations with Commonwealth African leaders. A senior official should be established in Salisbury to act as a regular channel of communication with Bishop Muzorewa. In the debate on The Queen's speech the Government should welcome the progress which had been achieved in Rhodesia and state that it wished to build on what had taken place to achieve the objective—a return to legality—with the best possible chance of securing wide international recognition. This involved consultation with our allies and the Commonwealth Governments concerned.

5. Lord Carrington had come to the conclusion that we must secure amendments to the Constitution. We should avoid any action which would disrupt the Commonwealth Heads of Government Meeting in August; but it would be necessary to complete our efforts to achieve a settlement before the Sanctions Orders came up for renewal in November.

6. The Government's first public pronouncement on Rhodesia was made in The Queen's speech on 15 May in guarded terms: 'Every effort will be made to end the conflict in Rhodesia and to bring about a lasting settlement based on the democratic wishes of the people of that country.'

In the debate on that day the Prime Minister said that it was the Government's objective to build on the major change which had taken place in Rhodesia to achieve a return to legality in conditions that secured wide international recognition. There would be consultations with the Nine, the Commonwealth and with the United States. 'We must and will take into account the wider international implications. I assure the House that we intend to proceed with vigour to resolve the issue'.

7. On 18 May the Lord Privy Seal said in the House of Commons that the Government had received Lord Boyd's report and it would be published. Lord Boyd's broad conclusion was that the election in Rhodesia was fair, in the sense that the electoral machinery was fairly conducted, that it was as free as was possible in the circumstances and that the result represented the wishes of the majority of the electorate. It was absurd that the British Government, which had special responsibilities in Rhodesia, had no way of informing itself directly or making its views felt in Salisbury. The Government would therefore be making permanent arrangements for continuing consultations with Bishop Muzorewa. Senior officials would visit Salisbury as often and for as long as was necessary for this purpose. There would also be consultation with the African Governments principally concerned.

8. Despite the terms in which this was phrased, the reference to permanent arrangements for consultations with Bishop Muzorewa produced the immediate reaction from the Nigerian Military Government, which imposed an embargo on tenders from British firms for major Nigerian Government contracts. The Government for its part was determined to take due account of British interests elsewhere in Africa, but not to permit its Rhodesia policy to be dictated from Lagos or elsewhere.

9. On 17 May Sir Antony Duff assured Bishop Muzorewa in Salisbury of the Government's intention to work with him. He emphasised the need to bring the war to an end and to achieve maximum acceptance in Africa. Precipitate action by Britain would not help towards those objectives and would result in damage to British interests elsewhere. It might be that some damage was in the end inevitable; but it was clearly the British Government's business to limit it as much as possible. Bishop Muzorewa welcomed the advent of a Conservative Government and agreed to the appointment of a senior official, Mr Derek Day, to maintain contact with him. On his return Sir Antony Duff recommended that Lord Carrington should seek to agree with Mr Vance on an approach designed to bring Rhodesia to legal independence by building on the new Rhodesian Government and Constitution, while seeking such changes as might be necessary to attract the support of other African countries and an end to the war either by negotiations or by undermining support for the Patriotic Front.

10. In talks with Mr Vance on 21 May Lord Carrington said that Lord Boyd clearly thought that the Rhodesian elections had fulfilled the fifth principle. The Government considered that it had to honour the undertakings in the Conservative manifesto. It was not committed on the time-scale but there were strong political pressures. There was no prospect of renewing sanctions in November. Mr Vance said that the Americans recognised the new reality created by the elections. But the lifting of sanctions would alienate black Africa and increase the leverage of the Russians and Cubans. Reflecting discussions earlier in the day between US and British officials Mr Vance speculated about the possibility of some revision of the Constitution; an attempt to move the Salisbury Government towards some form of all-party conference (but without a blocking power for the Patriotic Front); and an election after such a conference under some form of international supervision.

11. On 22 May Lord Carrington said in the House of Lords that a new approach was required. Lord Boyd had concluded that the election was as free as was possible in the circumstances. Lord Carrington did not however commit himself to the proposition that the fifth principle had been fulfilled. He said that the Government would be guided by Lord Boyd's conclusions in seeking to build on the progress which had been made. It was our responsibility to try to bring Rhodesia to independence in conditions which would afford the country the prospect of a more peaceful future and the widest possible international recognition. There was a need to carry international opinion with us, just as much for Rhodesia's sake as for our own.

12. On 7 June President Carter announced the decision he was required to make on sanctions under the terms of the Case-Javits amendment. The President stated that he was convinced that the best interests of the United States would not be served by lifting sanctions. The new Constitution had not been submitted to the African electorate. It preserved European control over the army, police, judiciary and civil service and gave the white minority a veto over significant constitutional change. Representatives of the external parties had not been able to participate in the political process. The Rhodesian authorities had expressed their willingness to attend an all-party meeting, but had not indicated that they were prepared to negotiate seriously on all the relevant issues. The United States recognised the progress that had been made and would keep the question of sanctions under review. The President acknowledged that he did not have majority support in the Senate; but he considered that to lift sanctions would be contrary to international law and damaging to United States interests in Africa.

13. The generally negative tone of President Carter's statement contradicted Lord Boyd's conclusions. The Senate sought to add an amendment

to the Military Authorisation Bill calling for an immediate end to sanctions; but the House of Representatives passed an amendment to the Bill deferring any such action to 15 October. The Department concluded that if in due course Britain lifted sanctions there seemed little doubt that, under Congressional pressure, the United States would be obliged to follow suit. But they would not recognise the Rhodesian Government unless there were further changes of a kind which would help to render such action more readily defensible elsewhere in Africa.

4. Lord Harlech's Mission (June-July 1979)

1. The Prime Minister decided that the consultative mission to Africa should be carried out by Lord Harlech, who had served as Deputy Chairman of the Pearce Commission and could be expected to command the respect of the Commonwealth African Presidents. The Parliamentary Under-Secretary, Mr Richard Luce MP, visited West Africa to consult some of the leading moderate African Presidents and urge them to use their influence to avoid extreme resolutions being passed at the summit meeting of the Organisation of African Unity in July.

2. Lord Harlech visited Africa between 11 and 22 June. He saw the Presidents of Zambia, Tanzania, Botswana, Angola and Malawi, the Mozambican Foreign Minister, the Nigerian Chief of Staff and representatives of the Patriotic Front. The purpose was to judge what prospect there was of the 'front line' Presidents acquiescing in a settlement based on the change which had taken place in Rhodesia or on some further development of it; and to gauge the prospects of the Patriotic Front joining in some wider agreement which would take those developments as it starting point.

3. Lord Harlech took the line that successive British Governments had been committed to bringing Rhodesia to legal independence on the basis of the six principles. Political change had taken place in Rhodesia on lines which in the British Government's view could be argued to satisfy to a very large extent those principles. But the change had been criticised as not going far enough. The Government had genuinely not made up its mind about the next steps to be taken towards the objective of bringing Rhodesia back to legality with the widest possible international acceptance. We were not merely 'playing for time' until after the Commonwealth Heads of Government Meeting. Lord Harlech did not suggest that the Government was itself trying to establish further conditions which Rhodesia would have to satisfy. His concern was to try to draw out from those he met their view of what might need to be done.

4. Lord Harlech concluded that not one of the Governments whose leaders he met would give even tacit support if we granted Rhodesia independence on the basis of the *status quo*. There was a unanimous view that

a settlement must be seen to be British and not merely the legalisation of a solution which we, the colonial power, had played no part in working out. The two broad areas of concern were the Constitution and power structure; and the need for some further step which would either bring about a wider agreement among the parties or settle in some other way their conflicting claims to have the support of the people of Rhodesia.

5. It was clear that there could be little hope of gaining wider acceptance of a Rhodesian Government which included Mr Ian Smith. There was general concern about certain features of the Constitution. There were precedents for temporary special representation for the whites in Parliament in other constitutions we had granted at independence. But there was strong resistance to the power given to the whites to block constitutional changes of their own. There was concern also about the lack of governmental control over the armed forces and police and about the powers of the white dominated commissions controlling senior appointments in the armed forces, police, judiciary and civil service.

6. It was repeatedly put to Lord Harlech that the new Constitution had not been submitted to a test of its acceptability to the African electorate. This question was linked with that of a possible wider agreement between Bishop Muzorewa and the external parties. There was probably no chance that a meeting of all Rhodesian parties could produce agreement on an independence constitution. But to convene such a conference might be a necessary step towards proposing a constitution acceptable to us and the Salisbury parties.

7. Lord Harlech considered that we should not despair of an internationally acceptable solution which would take *de facto* as its starting point the present settlement but

(*a*) such a solution would have to be recognisably British,

(*b*) it would have to include some amendment of the *status quo* including the departure of Mr Smith and elimination of the white veto in Parliament and

(*c*) there would have to be some means of neutralising the claims of the Patriotic Front through an attempted negotiation, a test of acceptability; a new election or some combination of these elements.

8. On 20 June the South African Foreign Minister, Mr Pik Botha, invited himself to London to see Lord Carrington. The South African Government were at this time developing the idea of a 'constellation' of neighbouring states with close economic ties with South Africa and well-disposed African Governments. Rhodesia, Botswana and eventually Namibia, it was hoped, would eventually conform to this pattern. The Salisbury Government were heavily dependent on South African financial and

military support and would not be prepared to risk forfeiting it. It was essential to secure South African acquiescence in our attempts to achieve a settlement.

9. Mr Botha argued strongly that if Britain took the lead in recognising Bishop Muzorewa's Government, much of Africa would follow suit. The situation inside the country was critical. If we did not move quickly to lift sanctions it would not be possible for South Africa to go on shouldering the burden of financial and other forms of support.

10. Lord Carrington said that the Government had a great deal of sympathy for Bishop Muzorewa. It was our objective to see a moderate and stable Government in Rhodesia, curtailing the possibilities for Soviet involvement and enabling the whites to stay. But he made clear that we were engaged in a process of consultation and did not intend to be rushed.

11. On 1 July the Prime Minister said at a press conference in Canberra that sanctions would lapse in November and it was doubtful whether a renewal of sanctions would go through the British Parliament. Although no more than a statement of political reality, this provoked an outcry in Africa.

12. In a memorandum to his ministerial colleagues on 2 July (OD(79)11) Lord Carrington said that Lord Harlech's consultations showed that a solution stemming purely from the settlement would not attract the support even of the most favourably disposed African Presidents. There was a general demand that we should make our own proposals for a solution and that the eventual independence Constitution should be seen to stem from Britain. As the constitutionally responsible authority we could not in any event disclaim responsibility for the constitutional arrangements under which Rhodesia was brought to legal independence. We could hope to achieve a settlement which would command a wider measure of international acceptance by

(*a*) persuading Bishop Muzorewa's Government to accept changes to the Constitution

(*b*) attempting to reach agreement on those changes and, in the likely event of Patriotic Front intransigence, demonstrating that it was the Patriotic Front who were the obstacle to a wider settlement.

13. We should aim for a policy statement after the Commonwealth Conference that we had consulted widely in the Commonwealth and Africa and were now able to make our own proposals for a settlement. We should put forward a broad outline of the main elements of an independence Constitution, based on the present Constitution, but with a reduction in the number of white seats and their power to block constitutional amendment and changes in the defence and public services commissions. We should announce that we were convening a conference in September

to seek agreement on a constitution on these lines. When agreement had been reached we would go on to discuss how to assure ourselves that these proposals were acceptable to the people of Rhodesia and how the first elections under the independence Constitution should be conducted. The conference might break down on Patriotic Front intransigence. In that event we would proceed with our constitutional proposals on the basis of acceptance by the internal parties.

14. The announcement that we would be making firm proposals to bring Rhodesia to legal independence with wide international acceptance would make the position clear before the Organisation of African Unity summit meeting from 16-19 July and the Commonwealth Heads of Government Meeting from 1-8 August. We should begin to seek Bishop Muzorewa's acquiescence in the eventual policy statement. We should seek the acquiescence of the Commonwealth Heads of Government in our general approach while not exposing our policy in such detail that they would have a chance to try to impose conditions or restraints. We should be prepared to demonstrate acceptability to the people of Rhodesia of what had been agreed. We should also ensure that Mr Smith honoured his promise to leave the Government. We should then grant legal independence to Rhodesia, lift sanctions and call upon other countries to follow suit. There could still be repercussions in Africa and the Commonwealth. But this course of action would give us the best basis to contain these, and a firm basis also on which to deal with other Commonwealth Governments at Lusaka.

15. Before the Cabinet discussion Lord Harlech saw Bishop Muzorewa in Salisbury on 3 July. He assured him that the British Government would not allow any extreme party or Government to stand in the way of a fair and reasonable settlement which had a prospect of wide international support. There was widespread criticism of certain aspects of the Constitution and a wish for a final solution which derived its authority from Britain. Bishop Muzorewa argued that if we recognised, others would follow suit. Rhodesia had fulfilled the six principles: we were now seeking to impose new conditions. General Walls and Bishop Muzorewa agreed to refrain from any military operations into Zambia during the Commonwealth Conference. Bishop Muzorewa stone-walled on the question of constitutional change but Lord Harlech believed that, in order to be given the prize of recognition, the regime probably would agree to some changes.

16. Lord Carrington had decided that we would need to impose changes in the Constitution; to call a conference which would probably not produce general agreement; and to arrange a test of acceptability. This would not satisfy Zambia and Tanzania and the war would probably continue; but wide recognition could erode the position of the Patriotic Front.

17. The Government were concerned that the changes we contemplated to the Constitution should not go so far as to destroy white confidence. It had not at this stage blocked off the option, if we could not achieve a better result, of eventually declaring that Rhodesia had satisfied the six principles and must be given independence. There could be no question of the Government laying an order for the renewal of sanctions in November. But the strategy proposed offered the best prospect of securing a measure of international acceptance and containing damage to our interests.

18. It was realised that the constitutional changes we would be seeking, far from being cosmetic, were in fact fundamental. What was at issue, as Lord Harlech said, was genuine majority rule. There could be no guarantee at this stage that the Rhodesian Government, conscious of the difficulty of renewing sanctions in November, could be induced to accept such changes. There was certain to be strong resistance from Mr Ian Smith. The decision that the British Government should make its own proposals for the basis on which it would be prepared to recommend to Parliament the granting of legal independence to Rhodesia was fundamental to our future strategy.

19. In the House of Lords on 10 July Lord Carrington said that the Government now had closer contact and was in a better position to influence events in Rhodesia than at any time since UDI. We must do all we could to bring about a situation in which Rhodesia was able to live at peace with its neighbours. Lord Harlech's consultations had revealed a widespread feeling that a solution must stem from Britain. The greatest service we could render to the people of Rhodesia was to aim for a settlement which would command wide international acceptance and bring an end to the war. In deciding its policy the Government would attach particular importance to the discussions at the Commonwealth Heads of Government Meeting. But it was Britain which had the responsibility to find a proper basis on which to bring Rhodesia to legal independence. That responsibility was recognised by the rest of the international community, many of whom lost no opportunity to remind us of it. The Government had not yet come to final conclusions about the proposals it intended to make. But it was its intention when its consultations had been completed to make firm proposals stemming from the British Government as the constitutionally responsible authority to bring Rhodesia to legal independence. Those proposals would take account of what had already been achieved in Rhodesia and would be comparable with the terms on which we had granted independence to other countries in the Commonwealth. The Government was determined to take the opportunity which now presented itself to achieve a solution.

5. *The Approach to the Commonwealth Conference (July 1979)*

1. On 11/12 July Bishop Muzorewa visited Washington. At the Prime Minister's request President Carter and Mr Vance impressed on him the need to work with the British Government to achieve a settlement. They made clear that constitutional changes would be essential to win international acceptance; and that the Bishop should make a genuine attempt to negotiate with the Patriotic Front. They added that they could see no prospect of a normalisation of relations with Rhodesia's neighbours so long as Mr Smith remained in the Government. Bishop Muzorewa indicated privately that he was prepared to consider reducing the blocking power of the 28 white MPs, but emphasised the need to preserve white confidence.

2. At a meeting with Bishop Muzorewa in London on 13 July the Prime Minister said that the British Government recognised what had been achieved in Rhodesia. But it was clear from the consultations we had held with other Governments that, to attract international acceptance, the independence Constitution would have to be comparable to the Constitutions which the United Kingdom had given to other African countries at independence; and would have to be seen to have originated with and to have been approved by the United Kingdom. It was important to retain white confidence; but the powers of the public service commissions were excessive as was the ability of the white Members of Parliament to block constitutional change. If the British Government regarded revised constitutional arrangements as acceptable, they would not permit them to be blocked by anyone else. There could be no objection to the principle of special representation for the minority community. At the Commonwealth Heads of Government Meeting, the Prime Minister would say that the British Government would be making proposals for the constitutional basis for legal independence. Thereafter the British Government would invite Bishop Muzorewa and the Patriotic Front to a conference. If the Patriotic Front refused to attend, this would not give them a veto over progress to independence. There would then have to be a test of acceptability. Lord Carrington said that unless changes of this kind were made, no country of any importance would recognise Rhodesia, even if Britain had done so.

3. Bishop Muzorewa expressed appreciation of the new and positive attitude of the British Government. He still believed that if we decided to recognise his Government, many in Africa would follow a clear lead. The Prime Minister said that it was apparent from our consultations that this was not the case. Bishop Muzorewa expressed concern about white confidence, about a future test of acceptability and about the time-scale. Lord Carrington emphasised that if acceptable constitutional proposals could be agreed between Britain and Bishop Muzorewa, the Patriotic Front would not be allowed to exercise a veto.

4. In a memorandum to his Cabinet colleagues on 19 July (OD(79)21) Lord Carrington described the discussions the Prime Minister and he had held with Bishop Muzorewa. They had gained the impression that he would be prepared to consider constitutional change; but there would be resistance from the Rhodesian Front. We should aim to publish by mid-August outline proposals for the independence Constitution comparable with the terms on which independence had been granted to other Commonwealth countries. The Patriotic Front were likely to reject the proposals we made at the conference; but it was essential to demonstrate that it was their intransigence which was the obstacle to a wider agreement.

5. Lord Carrington annexed the draft of the British outline proposals for the independence Constitution, subsequently published after the Commonwealth Conference. This was compatible with the existing Constitution except in relation to:

(*a*) the power to appoint and dismiss Ministers, which would be vested in the Prime Minister

(*b*) a change in the proportion of the European seats

(*c*) the arrangements for amendment of the Constitution

(*d*) the power to make senior appointments in the public service and other services would be vested in the Prime Minister, having consulted the appropriate public service commissions.

6. The proposals would be issued simultaneously with an invitation to Bishop Muzorewa's Government and the external parties to attend a constitutional conference in London in September. The invitation would make clear that the objective was agreement on an independence constitution to be granted by Britain; and that our proposals indicated the sort of constitution we were prepared to enact and which we believed should be acceptable as a basis for legal independence (though if alternative arrangements could be agreed by all the parties, we should be prepared to accept them).

7. Immediately after the Commonwealth Heads of Government Meeting, we should begin to discuss in detail with Bishop Muzorewa and his officials the changes we had in mind, so as to be in a position to table fully worked out proposals at the Constitutional Conference. Our aim in Lusaka should be to secure the acquiescence of the Commonwealth Heads of Government in our general approach, while avoiding exposing our policy in such detail as to give them a chance to try to impose conditions or restraints. We should resist attempts by President Nyerere or others to involve us in negotiating specific proposals with the Commonwealth or arrangements for the transition to independence loaded in favour of the Patriotic Front. There would be a general desire to avoid a confrontation; and on this basis it should be possible to do so. The announcement that there

would be a Constitutional Conference should cut much of the ground from under the critics and it might be best to hold this back until the later stages of the discussion.

8. An annex to the paper examined the kind of change which would be necessary to the Rhodesian Constitution to render it more comparable to those granted at independence to other African countries. There were precedents for the special representation of minority communities in Parliament for a limited period after independence in Tanzania, Zambia and Kenya. But the situation in Rhodesia, where the whites had 28 seats out of 100 in the lower house and the power to block a wide range of constitutional and other bills, was without precedent elsewhere. It was proposed to reduce the white seats to 20 per cent of the total, with 70 or at most 75 per cent of the votes to be required for constitutional amendment or other major measures.

9. There was a need for amendments to attenuate European dominance of the commissions controlling appointments to the public service, police, defence forces and judiciary; to open up the way for progressive Africanisation; and to give the Prime Minister power over the selection and retention of his senior officials and service commanders. The Constitution made a coalition Government obligatory for the life of the first Parliament and entitled every group with more than five MPs to automatic representation in the Cabinet. The Prime Minister had to accept the parties' nominations for Cabinet seats: he had no power to dismiss Ministers. It would also be desirable to amend the Constitution to make it easier to acquire land, with adequate compensation for existing owners, for settlement by Africans.

10. A separate paper examined in more detail the possible consequences for British political and commercial interests in the event of a Rhodesia settlement actively opposed by the majority of African states. In 1978 British exports to African countries totalled £2.8 billion (7.5 per cent of our total exports). The balance of trade in our favour was £1,252 millions. We had investment worth at least £1.25 billion in Africa. Although there was a strong likelihood of action against our interests in other African countries the real difficulties were likely to be faced in Nigeria and Zambia. The Nigerian military government had already imposed a selective embargo on the award of major Government contracts to British firms and were reported to be working on contingency plans for further action against British interests. If a serious confrontation developed over Rhodesia, the interests of Shell and BP in Nigeria would be affected. Nigeria might adopt a more moderate attitude after the return to civilian rule in October. Zambia was an important source of the United Kingdom's supplies of copper and cobalt; but the main danger in Zambia was the likeli-

hood of repercussions affecting the 29,000 strong British community involving the worst case their evacuation. Action against our interests in countries like Mozambique and Tanzania would be of more limited consequences.

11. By this time Bishop Muzorewa seemed to have taken in the case for changes to the Constitution. It remained probable that the Patriotic Front would reject our proposals. In that event we should have to negotiate these with the Bishop's Government and defend them internationally as being comparable to the terms with which other British colonies had been brought to independence; and arrange a test of acceptability. Some damage to our interests would be inevitable, particularly in Nigeria; but by this course we could hope to avoid wider political and economic damage.

12. The economic benefit of Rhodesia of sanctions being lifted would be great if others followed our example, but not if we acted almost alone. In the worst case, we might have to cope with a major rescue operation. The Government decided to aim for constitutional changes affecting particularly the blocking power of the whites and public service commissions, though without too radical a reduction in the preparation of white seats.

13. On 25 July the Prime Minister said in the House of Commons that what had been achieved in Rhodesia had brought us much closer to a solution than ever before. But it was imperative to seek one which contributed to a better and more secure future for the people of Rhodesia and the neighbouring territories. Lord Harlech had found criticism of certain parts of the Rhodesian Constitution and a general view that a solution must stem from Britain. The Commonwealth Heads of Government Meeting was a further important step in the process of consultation. Subsequently the British Government would put forward firm proposals on the constitutional arrangements to achieve a proper basis for legal independence for Rhodesia. In doing so they would be guided by the six principles and would aim to make the proposals comparable to the basis on which we granted independence to other former British territories in Africa. They would be addressed to all the parties to the conflict. The British Government were wholly committed to genuine black majority rule in Rhodesia. They believed that it was possible to reconcile reasonable assurance for the white community and the protection of their rights with genuine majority rule. They rejected the view expressed by Mr Nkomo to Lord Cledwyn-Hughes that there could only be a settlement by military means.

14. Despite the statements the Nigerian Military Government continued to suspect that, after the Commonwealth Conference, we would recognise Bishop Muzorewa's Government. The military leadership were highly nationalistic and anxious to assert Nigeria's claims to leadership in Africa. On the eve of the Commonwealth Conference they announced the

nationalisation of British Petroleum's assets in Nigeria. While this was related to BP's involvement in the supply of oil to South Africa (with the Nigerians alleging, wrongly, that Nigerian oil was liable to be exported there), it appeared also to be designed to establish the kind of action Nigeria and other African countries might take if our Rhodesia policy was not to their liking. Lord Carrington, reacting strongly to the Nigerian decision and its timing, made it clear that the Government would not allow its Rhodesia policy to be dictated by third countries.

6. The Commonwealth Conference (August 1979)

1. At the Commonwealth Heads of Government Meeting in Lusaka the discussion of Rhodesia was opened on 3 August by President Nyerere who said that there had been political changes in Rhodesia but these did not involve a real transfer of power to the majority. In many African countries there had been special provision for minority representation in Parliament at independence but it was unacceptable that the minority should control the judiciary, the public services, the police and the armed forces. The first requirement was for a democratic constitution. The second was that the Government assuming power under such a constitution should be chosen in a free election.

2. The Prime Minister in her opening statement said that the changes which had taken place in Rhodesia could not be dismissed as of no consequence. It was not reasonable to go on treating Bishop Muzorewa as if he were Mr Smith. We must use the opportunity created by those changes to see if we could now find a solution and bring an end to the war. From our consultations it was clear that it was widely felt that the constitution under which Bishop Muzorewa had come to power was defective in certain important respects—in particular the power of the white minority to block constitutional changes. This was a valid criticism: such a blocking mechanism did not appear in any other independence constitution agreed to by the British Parliament. The principle that there should be guaranteed representation for minority communities for a period after independence was not new. It was clearly wrong that the Government should not have adequate control over certain senior appointments. Those we had consulted also considered it essential that the search for a solution should involve the external parties. There was a general conviction that any solution must derive its authority from Britain as the responsible colonial power. The international community had lost few opportunities to remind us that it was our responsibility to bring Rhodesia to legal independence on a basis comparable with the arrangements we had made for the independence of other countries. We accepted that responsibility and had every intention of

discharging it honourably. The British Government were wholly committed to genuine majority rule. We accepted that it was our constitutional responsibility to grant legal independence on that basis and with a constitution comparable with the constitutions we had agreed with other countries. We were conscious of the urgent need to bring peace to the people of Rhodesia and its neighbours. We would therefore present our proposals to all the parties and call on them to cease hostilities and move forward with us to a settlement.

3. These speeches set the tone for a generally positive discussion, except for the intervention of the Nigerian Commissioner for External Affairs who said that if Nigeria were not satisfied with the outcome of the meeting, it would have to reconsider its membership of the Commonwealth. Following this discussion Presidents Kaunda and Nyerere and the Commonwealth Secretary General told the British delegation that they would like to establish a working group with the Prime Minister and Lord Carrington, Mr Fraser and Mr Manley, and the Nigerian Commissioner for External Affairs. This group worked out the following statement in the communiqué: 'In relation to the situation in Rhodesia, Heads of Government

- (*a*) confirmed that they were wholly committed to genuine black majority rule for the people of Zimbabwe;
- (*b*) recognised in this context, that the internal settlement constitution is defective in certain important respects;
- (*c*) fully accepted that it is the constitutional responsibility of the British Government to grant legal independence in Zimbabwe on the basis of majority rule;
- (*d*) recognised that the search for a lasting settlement must involve all parties of the conflict;
- (*e*) were deeply conscious of the urgent need to achieve such a settlement and bring peace to the people of Zimbabwe and their neighbours;
- (*f*) accepted that independence on the basis of majority rule requires the adoption of a democratic constitution including appropriate safeguards for minorities;
- (*g*) acknowledged that the Government formed under such an independence constitution must be chosen through free and fair elections properly supervised under British Government authority and with Commonwealth observers;
- (*h*) welcomed the British Government's indication that an appropriate procedure for advancing towards these objectives would be for them to call a constitutional conference to which all the parties would be invited; and,

(*i*) consequently, accepted that it must be a major objective to bring about a cessation of hostilities and an end to sanctions as part of the process of implementation of a lasting settlement.'

4. This draft was to have been submitted for approval to the other Heads of Government on 6 August. It was, however, leaked by the Australian delegation in terms which sought to give the impression that the Prime Minister had 'conceded' a constitutional conference and fresh elections. The communiqué was endorsed by the other Heads of Government at a barbecue given by Mr Fraser on 5 August. Nigerian agreement was given with considerable reluctance. The Prime Minister said that the agreement would be submitted for approval to the Cabinet on 10 August.

5. In Salisbury Bishop Muzorewa expressed satisfaction that the Commonwealth leaders had acknowledged the changes which had taken place in Rhodesia. But Lord Boyd and other observers concluded that the April elections would be free and fair. It was therefore insulting to insist that new elections must be held. Mr Day was instructed to point out that it was impossible to conceive of an independence constitution which did not provide for elections. There was also a strong and emotional reaction from the South African Government to the requirement of new elections. On the eve of the Conference Mr Pik Botha had sent a further message to Lord Carrington that if sanctions were not lifted forthwith Rhodesia would be in danger of imminent collapse. (These alarmist reports were partly attributable to a Rhodesian tendency, in their consultations with the South Africans, to exaggerate their difficulties in order to secure additional financial and military support). On 1 August Mr Botha sent a message to Lusaka that the Rhodesians were so incensed by President Kaunda's hostile remarks about Bishop Muzorewa that some military action was inevitable. This scare was purely of South African fabrication: General Walls assured us that he had no intention of authorising raids into Zambia during the conference.

6. On 6 August the Prime Minister told the press that the problem was to find a solution which would bring an end to the hostilities. If we had acted alone this would not have been of much help to Rhodesia. It was an enormous advantage to have got Commonwealth support and acceptance of Britain's responsibility. The Prime Minister, asked if we could provide troops in sufficient numbers to supervise the elections, replied that we did not anticipate any British troops going to Rhodesia. There would be pressure on the Patriotic Front to agree to the kind of constitution Britain had granted elsewhere. The Prime Minister refused to speculate about the possibility of a short period of direct British rule. But it would be culpable not to make the attempt to bring an end to the war. The Government had not performed a *volte face*. It had said from the outset that it must do its utmost

to ensure that the new independent state gained international recognition.

7. From Lusaka to Lancaster House (August-September 1979)

1. In a memorandum to his Cabinet colleagues on 9 August (C(79)33) Lord Carrington reported that the main features of the Lusaka Agreement were recognition of our constitutional responsibility to grant legal independence on the basis of majority rule with appropriate safeguards for minorities; and that it was for Britain to arrange supervision of fresh elections, with Commonwealth observers present. Our intention to call a constitutional conference was embodied in the Lusaka communiqué. The communiqué also drew attention to the fact that a Government formed under an independence constitution would have to be chosen through new elections. Such elections were essential to a settlement if it was to gain international acceptance and bring the war to an end. Lord Carrington proposed to issue invitations to the parties to attend a constitutional conference in September and to give them our outline proposals for an independence constitution on terms comparable to those on which independence was granted to other Commonwealth countries in Africa; which would offer enough protection to the whites to encourage them to stay; and which would be such that a refusal by the Patriotic Front to negotiate on that basis would be unreasonable. At the same time we would emphasise the importance we attached to enabling the white community to play a full part in the future of the country, and that legal independence would be granted and sanctions lifted once the proposals were implemented. We should avoid giving the Patriotic Front the chance to claim that we were aiming for a solution based on a modified version of the internal settlement; but our proposal would in many respects be compatible with the existing constitution.

2. Lord Carrington reported that on arrival the atmosphere in Lusaka had been unpromising. But it was clear that because of their own difficulties in the front line Presidents were anxious to see a settlement. President Nyerere had played a helpful role. Bishop Muzorewa would be told the details of the constitution we had in mind. Agreement with the Patriotic Front might not be possible, but if so we could hope to carry moderate opinion with us over the independence arrangements we would then reach with Bishop Muzorewa. If agreement were reached with all the parties there would be even greater difficulties to be overcome over the transitional arrangements, including the elections to which it had been necessary to agree in the Lusaka communiqué as the natural corollary of a new constitution; but these would be under British supervision and would be a price worth paying in order to end the war. The Prime Minister said that at Lusaka all Commonwealth Governments had accepted the primacy of

Britain's role. There had been no reference to the recognition by the Organisation of African Unity of the Patriotic Front as the sole representatives of the people of Rhodesia. It was agreed that the action proposed offered the best hope of progress. A number of questions were raised about the difficulties which might arise. But it was accepted that our policy could only be developed step by step. The Government should avoid hypothetical public discussion about their intentions in the event of failure; it was important to play for success and to be seen to be doing so.

3. Invitations were issued to Bishop Muzorewa and the Patriotic Front to bring delegations to a constitutional conference to be held at Lancaster House on 10 September. It was decided not to invite other parties or the representatives of sectional interests. The invitations stated that the purpose of the conference was to discuss and reach agreement on an independence constitution. The military questions associated with a transition to legal independence should be for discussion once the terms of an independence constitution had been agreed. Both sides were urged to agree to a cease-fire (though there was little hope of this being accepted in advance of a political agreement).

4. At the same time we published outline proposals for the independence constitution. These provided that the power to appoint and dismiss Ministers would be exercised in accordance with the advice of the Prime Minister. For a specified period after independence the House of Assembly would contain a minority of seats reserved for representatives elected by the European community. The proportion of those seats to the total number of seats in the House would be a matter for discussion. Parliament would have the power to amend the constitution on lines similar to those contained in other independence constitutions granted by Britain. The power to make senior appointments in the public service and other services would be vested in the Prime Minister. There would be a justiciable declaration of rights.

5. On 15 August Bishop Muzorewa's Government issued a statement agreeing to attend the conference on the understanding that there would be no preconditions. He was relieved to learn that there would be no participation by other Commonwealth Governments and that the composition of the Salisbury delegation would be for him to decide. He remained concerned about new elections. His party issued a statement welcoming our proposals and accepting the possibility of some constitutional change, though it was clear that some white officials were going to resist this. It was subsequently agreed that the composition of the Salisbury delegation should be based on the governing composition. Mr Ian Smith made it clear that he was determined to attend.

6. On 18 August the Patriotic Front rejected a cease-fire in advance of

the negotiations. Mr Mugabe stated that the Rhodesian army would have to be dismantled and replaced by Patriotic Front troops as part of the arrangements for the interim period. On 20 August the Patriotic Front leaders issued a statement agreeing to attend the conference but rejecting the proposed constitutional framework, the idea of special representation for the minority community and Britain's responsibility to ensure that new elections were fairly conducted. We pointed out to Commonwealth African Governments that this was incompatible with the Lusaka Agreement, which offered the only basis for a peaceful solution. We looked to them to support that Agreement and the constitutional proposals we had made in accordance with it; and to use their influence with the Patriotic Front to urge them to negotiate seriously on this basis.

7. On 21 August Mr Day and Mr Fifoot (a legal adviser in the Foreign and Commonwealth Office) explained to Mr George Smith, Secretary to the Rhodesian Cabinet, the changes we wished to see in the constitution. The proportion of white seats in the House of Assembly should be twenty per cent. Special white representation should be retained for a period shorter than ten years. The Prime Minister should have the right to dismiss any Minister from the Cabinet. Appointments to the office of Chief Justice, Permanent Secretary, Commissioner of Police or Commander of any branch of the defence forces should be made by the Prime Minister after consultation with the appropriate service commission. There should be provision for progressive Africanisation in the public service. Tenure of office by the Commissioner for Police and the military commanders should not be protected in the constitution. The requirements concerning the appointment of members of the public service commissions were too restrictive. Preventive detention outside a state of emergency should not be permitted. The white members of Parliament should not be able to block amendments to the constitution other than those affecting fundamental human rights or the number of white seats. With twenty per cent of seats held by the whites entrenched provisions should be capable of amendment by a seventy per cent majority. Consideration should be given to the introduction of a new constitution instead of merely amending the 1979 constitution.

8. On 24 August Mr Day was instructed to make clear to the Rhodesian authorities that, whatever internal procedures were followed, it was our intention that the independence Constitution should be enacted by the British Parliament. The Government would have to defend all aspects of the independence Constitution, which would not be accepted as legitimate unless it was enacted by us.

9. On 23 August Sir Antony Duff saw the South African Prime Minister in Pretoria. Mr P.W. Botha said that the British Government had executed

a *volte face*. Unless we could convince him that the whites would not be left in the lurch and the security forces would not be tampered with he could not guarantee South Africa's co-operation. A settlement must be achieved by the end of the year. Sir Antony Duff said that we would not allow the Patriotic Front to block an agreement we regarded as reasonable. After a difficult meeting, the conversation ended with Mr Botha saying that he would tell Bishop Muzorewa that, so long as he thought it in his interests to go along with the British plan, he should do so.

10. In a separate conversation the Secretary General in the South African Foreign Ministry, Mr Fourie, emphasised that Rhodesia was costing South Africa a great deal of money. Sir Antony Duff explained that sanctions would not automatically lapse in their entirety on 15 November. Mr Fourie though that Bishop Muzorewa would stand a good chance in new elections provided they were held without delay. The worst result would be a Government led by Mr Mugabe. The South Africans could not go on keeping Rhodesia afloat indefinitely if there were no prospects of change in the situation there.

11. It was no less important to guard against a tendency to retreat from the Lusaka Agreement—or to add to it—by the Commonwealth African Presidents. On 25 August President Nyerere wrote to the Prime Minister that the white MPs in the future Rhodesian Parliament should be elected by the entire electorate and not only the whites. It was vital that Britain should not go to the constitution conference as a 'neutral' arbitrating between the contending groups. Britain should act as the decolonising power, seeking as much agreement as possible but determined to transfer power to people elected under a democratic constitution. He wondered how the British Government could secure sufficient real authority on the ground to supervise the elections. He could not urge the Patriotic Front to accept arrangements for elections under those at present exercising authority in Rhodesia.

12. On 30 August the Prime Minister replied that we had to have regard to the reality of the situation in Rhodesia. We did not consider it unreasonable that, for a limited period after independence, the Europeans should elect their own representatives, though they should not have the power to block a wide range of legislation. The British Government did indeed intend to act at the Conference as the decolonising power. The first task would be to reach agreement on the independence constitution. 'We are deliberately—adopting a step by step approach: unless we seek to build up areas of agreement before moving on to tackle other tasks, we shall get nowhere'. If there was a measure of agreement on our outline of proposals for the constitution, we should be ready to bring forward more detailed proposals. Thereafter we could move on to discuss the manner in which

the constitution should be implemented. The essential point must be acceptance by the parties of new elections, supervised under the British Government's authority. Commonwealth observers would be present to see how this was carried out. The arrangements for new elections must permit the parties to participate in them with an equal chance of success. The success of the conference was likely to depend on the influence President Nyerere and other Commonwealth African leaders were prepared to exert. It would be extremely difficult to get Bishop Muzorewa and his colleagues to accept different constitutional arrangements on the key issues and new elections. There would be no chance of agreement if the Patriotic Front continued to reject our constitutional proposals and elections supervised under our authority. Mr Mugabe was already saying that he expected the conference to fail. The British Government were determined to transfer power on the basis of a democratic constitution. 'Both sides will I hope realise that it is likely to be costly for them if they seek to frustrate a political solution on these lines.'

13. On 1 September President Nyerere replied that, if it was clear that no-one would be allowed to exercise a veto over democratic decolonisation, this would assist in getting agreement. He would back up a British assertion of our authority and would make clear to the Patriotic Front leaders at the non-aligned conference in Havana that a failure to co-operate in the implementation of a democratic constitutional process would—as the Prime Minister had said—be very expensive. In general there was a fair measure of acceptance among Commonwealth African Governments of our policy of seeking agreement on the constitution before dealing with the problems of the transition. It was subsequently learned that Presidents Nyerere and Machel told the Patriotic Front leaders in Havana that they expected them to negotiate seriously at Lancaster House.

8. The Lancaster House Conference:
Negotiations on the Constitution (September-October 1979)

1. At the end of August Lord Carrington sent a minute to the Prime Minister (PM/79/74). This made clear that we were not approaching the Conference on the assumption that an overall settlement was likely to be attainable, though that should be our objective. Mr Smith's insistence on attending would give a propaganda advantage to the Patriotic Front. The initial Rhodesian reactions about constitutional change showed that there was tough bargaining ahead. The chances of the Patriotic Front accepting reasonable constitutional proposals and participating in new elections were not good, though Mr Nkomo would be under more pressure to settle than Mr Mugabe. It was more probable that we should be able to agree on

an independence constitution with Bishop Muzorewa which we could implement if it was demonstrated to be acceptable to the people of Rhodesia. We should not, however, proceed in such a way as to give rise to accusations that this was our objective from the outset. If there was a breakdown at the Conference, the responsibility should be clearly seen to rest with the Patriotic Front and their intransigence on the basic issues. There was support for the approach we had adopted that we must proceed step by step and the first task must be to secure agreement on the constitution.

2. Lord Carrington advised that although large sections of the existing constitution were unexceptionable, it would be prejudicial to the chances of agreement if we simply tabled the existing Rhodesian constitution, with amendments to it. We should allow the Conference to open with our outline proposals and seek to oblige the parties to declare their positions on them. We should then table a full outline constitution. This should be compatible with the existing constitution, apart from the areas we had already indicated we would insist on amending. We should then put forward proposals on the key issues of white representation, the blocking mechanism and the public service commissions. The proposal that 20 per cent of the parliamentary seats should be reserved for the white electorate would be criticised in Africa, but was indispensable to retain the confidence of the white community.

3. We should also be pressed to state how we intended to give effect to the commitment in the Lusaka Agreement to hold elections. We should say that once agreement had been reached on the fundamental question—the independence constitution—the Conference should move on to discuss the means of implementing it. If the Conference appeared to have reached a deadlock we should urge the Commonwealth African Presidents to intervene with the Patriotic Front. We should in the meantime proceed with bilateral negotiations with the Salisbury parties to establish the kind of constitution we could in the end accept. They would try to hold out for a settlement involving minimum changes. If we were to proceed with the internal parties we must be able to demonstrate the acceptability to the people of Rhodesia of what had been agreed. This meant that there would need to be a referendum or new elections on the basis of the independence constitution and that this test of acceptability must be supervised or a least observed by the British Government. This approach should enable us to retain as long as possible the support of the Commonwealth African Presidents—though it remained to be seen if they would be prepared to put effective pressure on the Patriotic Front. If the Patriotic Front rejected our proposals, we should be best placed to proceed with the internal parties with a chance of securing a measure of support at any rate from our principal friend and allies.

4. The opening of the Conference on 10 September was preceded by objections from the Patriotic Front to the seating arrangements, based on their insistence that Bishop Muzorewa should be considered part of the British delegation. Lord Carrington made it clear that he would open the Conference as planned whether or not the Patriotic Front attended the opening session.

5. The Conference opened with all delegations present. Lord Carrington said that there was a difference between this meeting and previous discussion of the Rhodesia problem. This was a formal constitutional conference. Our approach would be based on the same principles as those which had led to the decolonisation of other British colonies as the result of conferences at Lancaster House. He reminded the delegates of the terms of the Lusaka Agreement and the extent of Commonwealth support for a settlement. The people assembled in the conference room had it in their power to end the war. Neither side had infinite resources. The people of Rhodesia would not readily forgive any party which deprived them of this opportunity to settle their future by peaceful means. The constitution was the fundamental problem to which they must address themselves. If agreement could be reached on the independence constitution, it would be necessary to decide the arrangements to bring it into effect. The British Government would accept its full share of the responsibility in the implementation of those arrangements. The central element would be free and fair elections supervised under our authority. If it was possible to get agreement on the general framework of the independence constitution, we would be prepared to put forward more detailed proposals. In other countries approaching independence the United Kingdom's role had invariably been to establish just conditions for independence and not to encourage the aspirations of this or that party. In many countries we had handed over power to people who had previously been confirmed opponents of the policy of the United Kingdom, if they had been elected by the people of that country. He invited the other delegations to set out their views on the constitutional issues and our outline proposals.

6. In reply Mr Nkomo emphasised that stage which had been reached in the armed struggle and raised a series of questions concerning the exercise of power over and composition of the armed forces, civil service, etc. The British constitution proposals were too vague for the Patriotic Front to form a judgement on them. Bishop Muzorewa said that the six principles had already been fulfilled: it was now the duty of the British Government to grant legal independence and lift sanctions.

7. The Patriotic Front argued that discussion of the transitional arrangements should precede that of the constitution. On 12 September they submitted an agenda in the following sequence:

(1) Administration of country during transitional period
(2) Transitional constitution
(3) Independence constitution
(4) Cease-fire agreement.

Lord Carrington insisted that discussion of the independence constitution should take place first. He circulated the following agenda:

(1) Independence constitution
(2) Pre-independence arrangements including
　　(*a*) elections
　　(*b*) a cease-fire and military arrangements
　　(*c*) the administrative arrangements and the maintenance of law and order during the transitional period.

This involved over-ruling Bishop Muzorewa as well as the Patriotic Front: the Salisbury delegation were objecting at this stage to discussion of any issues other than the constitution. Lord Carrington made it clear that if agreement was reached on an independence constitution, the Conference would go on to discuss the arrangements for implementing it. At the same time, in order to advance the discussion, Lord Carrington circulated a fuller summary of our proposals for the independence constitution. On 14 September Bishop Muzorewa's delegation circulated as a counter proposal the existing Zimbabwe-Rhodesia constitution. The Patriotic Front tabled their own proposals, including an executive President and an Assembly with no reserved seats for the white community.

8. On the same day Mr Ian Smith and some other members of Bishop Muzorewa's delegation sought a meeting with the Secretary of State. Lord Carrington said that it would be very difficult to get through Parliament a Bill granting independence on the basis of the existing constitution. It was a mistake to believe that sanctions would lapse automatically in November. The Prime Minister had said at Lusaka that the Rhodesian constitution was defective in certain important respects. If, however, the Salisbury delegation agreed to and the Patriotic Front rejected an acceptable independence constitution, we would go ahead with the Salisbury parties. But every effort must be made to reach agreement. Mr Smith said that there could be no protection for the white minority without a blocking power.

9. As it had become apparent that the tactics of some of the Rhodesian Front Ministers would be to try to push us up against the deadline for the renewal of sanctions in November while rejecting any constitutional change or seeking to settle for purely cosmetic amendments, a fuller explanation of our sanctions legislation was given with Lord Carrington's approval to Rhodesian officials. They were told that if Section 2 of the Southern Rhodesia Act 1965 was not renewed in November, positive action would still be required to revoke the orders under the Defence (Import,

Export and Customs) Act 1939, the United Nations Act 1946 and restrictions under the Exchange Control Act 1947. The changes to the exchange control regulations would have to be laid before Parliament. While the revocation of orders did not necessarily require parliamentary action, because their removal would be in violation of Britain's treaty obligations, the Government would certainly have to face a vote on the issue in Parliament.

10. On 14 September President Nyerere told the Prime Minister that he did not think the Conference would break down on the constitution. He did not see major difficulty in the Patriotic Front accepting reserved white seats. But the Conference would have to take up the question of the interim arrangements at an early stage. The Prime Minister said that there would have to be a cease-fire and separation of the forces. President Nyerere said that he would not back a settlement which did not provide for the integration of the forces before independence. Sir Antony Duff said that it would be impossible to achieve agreement at this stage on the creation of a single army. President Nyerere suggested that if Bishop Muzorewa lost the election, the South Africans would intervene. The Prime Minister asked whether it was realistic to suppose that in the aftermath of an election the losers would be able to continue to struggle. President Nyerere asked whether we were prepared to put in British troops or organise a Commonwealth force.

11. It was essential to prevent President Nyerere seeking to establish new conditions for a settlement and thereby under-cutting any chance of a successful negotiation. Following this conversation, we explained to other Commonwealth African Presidents our view that to try to resolve the problem of the integration of the armed forces in advance of the fundamental political decision on the future Government in free elections was impracticable. It transpired that Presidents Kaunda and Machel were more conscious of the practical impossibility of integrating the armies before elections were held.

12. On 18 September the Patriotic Front stated that meaningful discussions on an independence constitution could not be held without dealing with the fundamental issues involved in the transition to independence. They put forward a plan for an eight member governing council and a six-month transition period, with a UN peace-keeping force. The governing council would have four representatives from the Patriotic Front, three from the internal parties and a British Chairman without a casting vote. The Patriotic Front proposals were more moderate than any they had put forward in previous negotiations, revealing the pressure they were under to adopt a reasonable attitude. Their proposals for the governing council would, however, have resulted in deadlock. Lord Carrington insisted that

the agreement must be reached on the independence constitution before moving on to tackle the pre-independence arrangements.

13. From 19 September to 2 October no plenary sessions were held. At a first bilateral meeting with Bishop Muzorewa's delegation on 19 September Mr Smith said that most of the countries giving Britain advice were dictatorships. There was a strong chance that the United States would remove sanctions and that would solve Rhodesia's problem. He was not impressed about the consequences of failure of the Conference. The concessions we were asking for would interfere with the rights secured for whites in the present constitution. Mr Sithole made it clear that Mr Smith's views did not reflect those of other members of the delegation, though there was more general resistance to the idea of new elections. At a meeting with the Salisbury delegation on 20 September there was a long argument with Mr Ian Smith and Mr Anderson about minority representations and the blocking mechanism. Lord Carrington pointed out that the whites, who represented three per cent of the population, were being offered twenty per cent of the parliamentary seats. A seventy per cent majority would be required for constitution amendment but basic human rights of interest to all citizens of the independent state would be entrenched in a Declaration of Rights which could be amended only by a unanimous vote of the Assembly.

14. In a further bilateral meeting on 21 September Mr Ian Smith sought a guarantee that once agreement on the constitution had been reached, sanctions would be lifted immediately. Lord Carrington said that sanctions would be lifted as part of the process of implementing an agreement and a return to legality. Mr Anderson asked whether the number of white seats and the percentage required for constitutional amendment were negotiable. He was told that they were not.

15. These meetings were accompanied by intensive discussions with key members of Bishop Muzorewa's delegation outside the Conference. We were assisted by the fact that Bishop Muzorewa, through his private secretary, Dr Kamusikiri, was ready to work with us to achieve the constitutional changes we were seeking, as were Dr Mundawarara and the Rev Sithole. Mr Flower and Air Vice Marshal Hawkins were also working hard to achieve a settlement, despite the misgivings of other white officials. Among the Rhodesian Front Ministers, Mr David Smith strongly favoured a settlement, not least because he could otherwise see little prospect of continuing to finance the war. Mr Rowan Cronje's attitude was important, because his backing was essential to Mr David Smith and because of his connections with the South Africans. He was won over gradually to acceptance of the need for constitutional change. Mr Anderson continued to support Mr Ian Smith.

16. On the evening of 21 September Bishop Muzorewa's delegation announced that they accepted the main points of principle in our constitutional proposals. This decision was taken after a ballot of the delegation in which the voting was eleven to one in favour of acceptance, the dissenting voice being that of Mr Ian Smith. The acceptance was contingent on satisfactory detailed arrangements being worked out and on agreement on the subsequent process of implementation.

17. In bilateral discussions with the Patriotic Front Mr Nkomo continued to argue that to provide for the election of white MPs by the white electorate was a racialist provision. The Patriotic Front did not, however, contest separate representation for the white community as vigorously as had been expected—reflecting pressure from President Machel and others. In a breakthrough on 24 September they agreed to the proposal that twenty per cent of the seats in the Assembly should be reserved for whites elected by the white community.

18. A series of bilateral meetings at official level with the Salisbury delegation were conducted by Sir Antony Duff. Bishop Muzorewa's delegation fielded their principal legal experts. Sir Antony Duff said that the British Government would have to defend in Parliament and internationally the entire text of the independence constitution. It would therefore be necessary to review all the provision of the 1979 Constitution. There followed a series of difficult discussions in which some of the Rhodesian officials sought, without success, to minimise the changes which would be necessary. On 26 September the Department reported that the main difficulties which had arisen concerned:

(*a*) the period for which the white seats would be entrenched;

(*b*) the demand that the whites should be able to vote on both electoral rolls;

(*c*) the composition of the Senate (the one third reserved for Chiefs);

(*d*) we were concerned to remove from the Declaration of Rights provision for preventive detention outside a state of emergency: to provide for the acquisition with compensation of under-utilised land: and to reduce the extent of the savings in a state of emergency and the validation of existing laws even when in contravention of the Declaration of Rights.

19. On the same day Mr Nkomo and Mr Mugabe called on Lord Carrington. The main unresolved constitutional issues with the Patriotic Front concerned:

(*a*) citizenship—the Patriotic Front wanted to be able to weed out 'undesirables'. They were told that this was unacceptable to us;

(*b*) they wanted white representation for five years only and an improvement in the composition of the Senate;

(*c*) they would not discuss the constitutional arrangements concerning the defence forces, police and judicature until their composition had been decided during the transitional period;

(*d*) they objected to the pensions of public servants being guaranteed by the constitution;

(*e*) they wanted existing judges and magistrates and certain senior officials to vacate their offices before independence.

The Patriotic Front were, however, weakening in their insistence on an executive Presidency: Mr Mugabe had less enthusiasm for this than Mr Nkomo. Mr Nkomo asked if our final constitutional proposals would be presented on a take it or leave it basis. Lord Carrington emphasised that our proposals were already a compromise: we had insisted on major changes from the existing constitution. Mr Mugabe said that the Patriotic Front would not agree to the constitution until the transitional arrangements had been discussed. Lord Carrington said that the constitution could not be reopened after discussion of the transitional arrangements. Agreement to the constitution could, however, be contingent on agreement on the pre-independence arrangements.

20. On 1 October Lord Carrington held a final meeting on the constitution with Bishop Muzorewa and his delegation. He said that we could not agree that the whites should vote on the common roll as well as on the white roll. Mr Ian Smith and Mr Anderson argued strongly that power over the appointment and dismissal of the judges, senior civil servants and service commanders must remain outside governmental control, with Mr Smith claiming that the service commanders were opposed to any change. Concern was expressed about the provisions to enable the Government to take over under-utilised land and about pension rights. Lord Carrington said that Britain could not guarantee the pensions of Rhodesian civil servants.

21. On the same day Lord Carrington saw Mr Nkomo and Mr Mugabe. Mr Nkomo expressed concern that if, having agreed a constitution in principle, the Patriotic Front then failed to agree on arrangements for the interim period, we would implement the new constitution with the Salisbury parties alone. Lord Carrington said that, having discussed all the issues, we had to advance the work of the Conference. We therefore intended to table our full constitutional proposals and seek a final response to them.

22. At a bilateral meeting on 2 October the Patriotic Front argued that the provision in the Declaration of Rights concerning protection from arbitrary deprivation of property should not prevent the elected Government from redistributing land. They criticised the proposal that the main provisions in the Declaration of Rights should be amendable only by a unanimous vote in the House of Assembly as a restriction on the sovereignty of

Parliament. Lord Carrington replied that our proposals would not prevent the Government from implementing a fair policy of land resettlement. The entrenchment of the Declaration of Rights was intended to reassure all the citizens of Zimbabwe that fundamental human rights would be protected.

23. On the afternoon of 2 October plenary sessions of the conference resumed. Mr Nkomo, abandoning his previous refusal to negotiate with the Salisbury delegation, made a vain attempt to draw them into discussion of various points of the constitution (probably in the hope that the Rev Sithole, with whom he maintained contact throughout the Conference, might be induced to break ranks with Bishop Muzorewa). Mr Mugabe complained about the bilateral sessions. The British delegation had apparently concluded an agreement with one party, whereas his delegation had not even agreed on broad principles. Lord Carrington recalled that at the start of the Conference the Patriotic Front had stated that they were prepared to negotiate only with the British delegation. It had been agreed that the only way to proceed was by means of bilateral meetings.

24. On 3 October Lord Carrington informed the Prime Minister of the full proposals he intended to table in the Conference that afternoon. The document was fully compatible with the proposals we had tabled at the beginning of the Conference and represented a wide measure of agreement with the Salisbury delegation. It would serve as a comprehensive guide from which our legal draftsmen could prepare the final text of the constitution. It was still not clear whether the Patriotic Front would accept a constitution on these lines. They would criticise the provisions for citizenship, pensions, land, agricultural settlement and the entrenchment of the Declaration of Rights. But they could find themselves in considerable difficulty if the Conference broke down on their rejection of proposals which, to any reasonable observer, marked an enormous advance on any previous attempt to achieve a constitutional settlement for Rhodesia.

25. In the bilateral negotiations with the Salisbury delegation we had been able to achieve all our main objectives, and to ensure that in addition to the fundamental changes which were required to make provision for genuine majority rule, a number of consequential and other changes were accepted which rendered the final text of the independence constitution a document which in all respects we could justify in Parliament and elsewhere. These negotiations imposed a considerable strain on the participants. The Conference was turning into a test of the stamina of all three delegations.

26. In the Conference on 3 October, Lord Carrington put forward a full description of the independence constitution which we intended to recommend to Parliament. This, he said, could not meet fully the differing requirements of the other delegations. Since the parties could not themselves

agree it was for us to make clear what we considered to be the basis for a constitutional settlement. To carry forward the Conference, we needed to know whether both delegations could accept such a constitution, subject to subsequent discussion of the arrangements for bringing it into effect. Lord Carrington asked both delegations to let him know by 8 October whether they could accept our proposals.

27. The Patriotic Front reacted strongly to this 'ultimatum'. Mr Ian Smith, on the other hand, was arguing that by giving the Government control over senior appointments, including the police commissioner and army commanders, we were turning the Prime Minister into a dictator; that our proposals would destroy the independence of the judiciary; and that they would undermine white confidence, particularly in the defence forces. Mr Smith intended to return to Salisbury to appeal to white opinion there against acceptance to our proposals.

28. To undercut Mr Smith's efforts to frustrate an agreement we continued discussions outside the Conference with the principal African members of Bishop Muzorewa's delegation, particularly Dr Mundawarara and Dr Kamusikiri, as well as with the key white members working for a settlement. Our objective at this stage was not only to secure agreement to our constitutional proposals but also to persuade the delegation to make the earliest possible statement of their agreement to new elections, thereby putting us in a strong position internationally and undercutting the Patriotic Front's argument that our intention was to agree to a new constitution with Bishop Muzorewa and then to implement it in a settlement from which they would be excluded. At the same time efforts were made by the Lord Privy Seal and other members of the British delegation to develop informal contacts with the Patriotic Front and to assure them of our determination to try to reach a settlement in which they could participate. These approaches met at this stage with a more positive response from ZAPU than from ZANU.

29. The commitment to new elections was still very difficult for Bishop Muzorewa to accept. There was strong resistance within his delegation and the South Africans were advising him not to do so. We had to work hard on all the more sympathetic members of the Salisbury delegation. Bishop Muzorewa's position was strengthened when, on behalf of the service commanders, General Walls assured him of his support and dissociated himself from Mr Ian Smith's claim that the commanders would not accept changes in the constitution. On 15 October Bishop Muzorewa announced his acceptance of our full constitutional proposals and new elections to be supervised under our authority. The decision was taken by a majority of eleven to one, the dissenting voice again being that of Mr Ian Smith who left immediately for Salisbury.

30. On 8 October the Patriotic Front tabled counter proposals accepting a constitutional Presidency and the proposed composition of the legislature (including the Senate), but maintaining their reservations in relation to citizenship, pensions, the Declaration of Rights, etc. Mr Nkomo argued that despite his delegation's reservations, the Conference should go on to deal with the pre-independence arrangements. Lord Carrington said that we had made it clear from the outset that we would not be prepared to open discussion on the pre-independence arrangements until agreement had been reached on the Constitution.

31. On 9 October Bishop Muzorewa told the Lord Privy Seal that he was proceeding on the assumption (as he did throughout the Conference) that the Patriotic Front would take part in the elections. He would prefer to see a settlement that would end the war. The Patriotic Front would maintain their unity until the Conference was over; but it was now entering a more difficult phase and it was hard to see on what basis agreement could be reached.

32. On the same day Lord Carrington told the Patriotic Front that the differences which remained were fundamental and could not be left on one side. All the issues had been discussed exhaustively. The proposals we had made were in our judgement the only basis on which it was possible to reach agreement. We could not proceed with discussion of the pre-independence arrangements while either side reserved the right to re-open substantive issues on the constitution.

33. The Conference adjourned for a day to enable the Secretary of State to address the Conservative party conference in Blackpool. In his speech Lord Carrington said that if we had acted alone to recognise Bishop Muzorewa's Government, no-one would have followed us. There would have been no chance of ending the war. At Lancaster House there could not be a repetition of the empty haggling at Geneva. There must now be a decision on the constitution. It was not feasible to integrate the armed forces or to make other radical changes before elections were held. The time for the lifting of sanctions could not now be far off; but we were at present in the midst of a difficult negotiation. No-one, however, would be allowed to decide unilaterally that Rhodesia must continue in illegality and isolation. 'What we are striving to do is to solve a tragic problem with honour, with dignity and with justice.' If there had been concern about the reactions in the Conservative party, this was dispelled by the reception his speech received. In her speech on the following day the Prime Minister emphasised what had been achieved at and since Lusaka and the British Government's duty to do everything in its power to bring an end to a war now rendered pointless by the attainment of genuine majority rule.

34. As the pressure increased on the Patriotic Front to agree to the constitution, their reservations began to be narrowed down to the question of land. Following contacts with the Commonwealth Secretary General and the Americans, Lord Carrington made a statement on 11 October intended to help them over this difficulty. We recognised that the future Government of Zimbabwe would wish to extend land ownership. The independence constitution made it possible to acquire under-utilised land provided adequate compensation was paid. The British Government would be prepared, within the limits of our financial resources, to help with schemes for agricultural development and to support the efforts of the independence Government to obtain international assistance for those purposes. Lord Carrington also assured the Patriotic Front that the white representatives could not form a coalition with a single African party to frustrate the wishes of the majority.

35. Mr Nkomo replied with a statement that except for such major issues as land, the Declaration of Rights insofar as it affected land and pensions, and the provisions relating to the army, police, public services and judiciary; the Patriotic Front were now satisfied that the Conference had reached a sufficiently wide measure of agreement on the independence constitution to enable it to proceed to the next item on the agenda. If they were satisfied on these issues in the transitional arrangements there might not be a need to revert to discussion on them.

36. Lord Carrington adjourned the Conference briefly in an attempt to obtain a clear statement from the Patriotic Front leaders as to whether they could accept the independence constitution. When it resumed he said that the Patriotic Front were making reservations on a number of issues which on their own admission were of major importance. We had tried to help them on the question of land. But the negotiations must proceed step by step if they were not to prove as fruitless as those in Geneva. The British Government could not accept the reservations in Mr Nkomo's statement. To do so would mean that major questions would be re-opened after discussion of the interim arrangements. When the Conference resumed this would be to discuss arrangements for implementing the independence constitution. Before then we needed to know whether the Patriotic Front could accept the constitution.

37. It was essential to obtain an unequivocal response both to give the Conference a firm basis on which to proceed and to avoid serious difficulties with and for Bishop Muzorewa, who was by now protesting strongly at the delay in proceeding to discussion of the pre-independence arrangements. His concern was increased by Mr Ian Smith's attempts in Salisbury to win the support of the 28 Rhodesian Front MPs for his opposition to the

constitutional proposals. Mr Smith also sought (without success) to persuade the service commanders to oppose them.

38. Lord Carrington asked Mr Nkomo and Mr Mugabe to call on him on 15 October and said that he was awaiting a definite answer on acceptance of the independence constitution. In a final effort to force the Patriotic Front over this hurdle—and to keep the Salisbury delegation at the Conference—Lord Carrington announced that evening that in view of the Patriotic Fronts' failure to accept the constitution, discussions about the arrangements to implement it would take place without their participation. They would be welcome to join these discussions as soon as they could indicate acceptance of the constitution. It remained our objective to work out pre-independence arrangements which would enable all parties to participate in free elections.

39. On 16 and 17 October bilateral meetings were held with Bishop Muzorewa's delegation to discuss the transitional arrangements. Lord Carrington made it clear that we would do nothing at this stage that would foreclose the possibility of the Patriotic Front participating. On 18 October he held a meeting with Mr Nkomo and Mr Mugabe, at which there was a further brief discussion of the land issues. Lord Carrington said that it was not our purpose to buy out the white farmers and that we could not agree to a 'land fund'; but there would be international assistance, with contributions from us and from the Americans, for agricultural development and settlement. The Patriotic Front leaders produced a draft statement, about which they had consulted Mr Ramphal, that in view of these assurances 'we are now able to say that if we are satisfied beyond doubt about the vital issues of the transitional arrangements, there will not be a need to revert to discussion on the constitution including these issues on which we reserved our position'. This statement was read into the Conference record on 19 October, enabling the Conference to proceed to discussion of the pre-independence arrangements.

9. The Pre-Independence Arrangements (October-November 1979)

1. On 28 September Lord Carrington reported to the Prime Minister and his ministerial colleagues that our proposals for the pre-independence period must be designed for a situation in which we had all-party agreement to proceed to elections, but adaptable for use if we had to go ahead with the Salisbury Government alone. They must safeguard our position in international law and demonstrate that the Patriotic Front had been given a fair chance to participate. If legality had not been restored by November we should be in difficulty over Section 2 of the Southern Rhodesia Act. The attraction for Bishop Muzorewa of a return to legality was that it

would enable us to lift sanctions forthwith. This should ensure the co-operation of the whites. The provision for elections and the independence
constitution would require an Act of Parliament.

2. The main question to which Lord Carrington addressed himself was
whether we should aim for a return to legality with a British Governor
assuming direct executive and legislative authority; or do so while leaving
the existing Government in place. He advised that the only arrangement
which would carry conviction with the international community would be
a British administrator with executive and administrative authority. The
aim would be to conduct the elections and proceed to independence within
at most twelve weeks. The administrator would confine his activities very
largely to what was strictly necessary for the electoral process including
supervision of the police. The present Government would stand aside with
Bishop Muzorewa concentrating on the electoral campaign. The administration would be carried on by Rhodesian civil servants. Such an arrangement would put pressure on the front line Presidents to push the Patriotic
Front into agreeing a cease-fire. The Patriotic Front would try to negotiate
with us the arrangements for control over the administration, etc, but we
should take firmly the line that this was our business. They would argue
that elections held with the existing administration and security forces in
place would put them at a disadvantage; and that there should be some
neutral force. But this approach would give us the best prospect of securing some international support, whether or not the Patriotic Front participated. We had begun to prepare the ground with some members of Bishop
Muzorewa's delegation—in particular Mr David Smith.

3. If the Patriotic Front participated, the main difficulty would be in
maintaining the cease-fire. A small military 'third force' might well be
necessary and could be a *sine qua non* for President Kaunda's support.
There would be no point in putting forward proposals in this area unacceptable to Bishop Muzorewa and the Rhodesian military commanders
and which could not therefore be implemented. We were exploring the
possibilities with General Walls.

4. If the Patriotic Front did not participate we would have to supervise
elections with the war continuing. We should be legally responsible for
the activities of the Rhodesian administration, including the armed forces.
We should have to get General Walls to give a firm assurance that, for the
period required to organise elections, military activity by the Rhodesian
forces *vis-à-vis* Zambia and Mozambique would be restricted to defence
from inside Rhodesian frontiers. There would be resistance in the United
Nations to the lifting of sanctions with a return to legality without the Patriotic Front. But we would hold open the invitation to their Front to participate. A full-scale return to legality would give us a respectable legal

argument in the Security Council while legalisation of the existing Government would not.

5. The main resistance to a return to legality on these terms would come from Mr Ian Smith. If the present Government remained in office, it would not be possible to attract international support, even if we appointed a British Election Commissioner. President Kaunda would be unlikely to put any pressure on Mr Nkomo to participate. Few countries would be prepared to follow our example in lifting sanctions. Lord Carrington concluded that in relation to the pre-independence arrangements, as over the constitution, we must retain the initiative and proceed on the basis of a firm British plan.

6. There began a long and difficult process of negotiation with the Salisbury delegation. We had already begun to discuss some of these ideas with Dr Mundawarara, Dr Kamusikiri, Mr David Smith, Mr Flower and AVM Hawkins. We emphasised that, in order to enable sanctions to be lifted from the outset of the process leading through elections to independence, there would be need to return to legality. The key question was the position of the Government in such circumstances. It was clear that if our role was restricted to supervising the elections the Patriotic Front would not participate and that other countries would not regard this as fair and equitable as between the parties participating in them.

7. In Salisbury the Rhodesian military commanders took the view that Bishop Muzorewa would put himself in a dangerous political disadvantage if he gave up his position as Prime Minister. They asked if we could not confine our role to supervising the elections, continuing the present Government in office, removing only the President and replacing him with a British nominee. On instructions Mr Byatt, who had been sent to Salisbury to maintain contact with the military commanders and others, said that a return to legality on this basis would carry little convictions with international opinion. General Walls remained concerned that, if Bishop Muzorewa stood aside, the South Africans would withdraw their military support. The military commanders were opposed to an advisory council and to anything which took executive authority out of the hands of the existing Government. They considered that a titular Governor was as far as it was safe to go. They proposed that the Governor should continue to run the country on a day to day basis but would not be concerned with anything to do with the elections or a cease-fire. The defence commanders would agree that no operations would be conducted outside Rhodesia or above company level inside Rhodesia without consultation with us. There would be a Council with a British Chairman to organise the elections.

8. In London African members of the Salisbury delegation were also strongly opposed to Bishop Muzorewa standing down. We continued to

argue that it would be impossible to convince international opinion that the Patriotic Front were being given a fair chance to participate in elections if the Government remained in the hands of Bishop Muzorewa and his Ministers. The Rhodesians indicated that Bishop Muzorewa and his Ministers might be prepared to detach themselves from the administration for the actual election campaign. We proposed that legislative and executive authority should be vested formally in a British Governor. The Bishop and his Ministers need not stand aside forthwith, but would have to be prepared to do so for the election campaign. The period in question should, however, be longer than that envisaged by the Rhodesians. The commanders would have to come formally under the authority of the Governor. It was agreed that General Walls and the Police Commissioner should come to London to carry forward these discussions.

9. On 13 October officials discussed with Dr Mundawarara and Air Vice Marshal Hawkins a draft paper envisaging a British Governor with military and police advisers. In the first stage Bishop Muzorewa and his Ministers would act as a caretaker Government. There would be an Election Council and a Cease-fire Commission. The Governor would be responsible for the arrangements concerning the elections. In the second stage all the political leaders would commit themselves to the election campaign. The Governor would be directly responsible for the administration of the country.

10. On 15 October the Lord Privy Seal discussed with Bishop Muzorewa the terms of a return to legality. It was made clear that whatever the attitude of the Patriotic Front, we would have to work out an arrangement which we could present to Commonwealth Governments and others designed to fulfil the Lusaka agreement and to enable the Patriotic Front to participate in elections if they were prepared to do so. The discussions with Bishop Muzorewa's representatives, were enlarged on 15 October to include General Walls and the Police Commissioner.

11. Bishop Muzorewa explained to his delegation that we envisage a British representative in Salisbury and a temporary return to the status of a British dependent territory. The present Governor would continue for a short time on a caretaker basis. The army and police forces would be left intact. The general response of the delegation was to ask why the Government should stand aside. Bishop Muzorewa nevertheless told us privately that he believed that, if we were able to proceed as we had done over the constitution, there was a reasonable prospect of ending up with only Mr Smith and Mr Anderson opposing our proposals. Bishop Muzorewa hoped that Lord Carrington would tell his delegation formally that, unless certain indispensable steps were taken, international recognition would not be forthcoming and the war would continue and intensify. We should not give

the impression that there was any 'give' in our position.

12. On 16 October Lord Carrington told the Salisbury delegation that he did not know whether the Patriotic Front would agree to the Constitution. He proposed to continue with them alone, but on the assumption that the Patriotic Front might come back later. It was essential to devise interim arrangements which would win international acceptance. New elections must be held to bring the independence constitution into effect. The Patriotic Front must be given the chance to participate, though the elections would go ahead whether they did so or not. We would not accept the Patriotic Front's proposals for the interim period, particularly as regards changes in the armed forces. An election should be held as soon as possible because a cease-fire, if one could be negotiated, would be fragile. We had in mind the appointment of an Election Commissioner to work with the Salisbury authorities in organising the elections and an Election Council in which all the participating parties would be represented. Mr Ian Smith said that the holding of the elections should be postponed until normality had returned to Rhodesia and terrorism and intimidation had died down. Lord Carrington said that our aim was to bring Rhodesia to independence; this must follow elections. Mr Anderson asked if sanctions would only be lifted after the elections. The Lord Privy Seal said that sanctions might be lifted before elections, depending on the interim arrangements, including the question of legality.

13. On 17 October the South African Foreign Minister came to London at the request of Mr P.W. Botha to see the Prime Minister. The South Africans had played a reasonably helpful role during the discussions on the constitution. They did not support Mr Ian Smith in his opposition to our proposals. Subsequently, however, the South African Prime Minister and Foreign Minister had both made public statements envisaging military intervention in Rhodesia in the event of a 'breakdown' in that country. The South Africans were putting pressure on Bishop Muzorewa not to hand over executive authority; and had told General Walls that this could affect their military supplies. Part of their concern was that our interim arrangements could affect their links with the Rhodesian forces. But their main objectives were to ensure that the Patriotic Front were not given a chance to win elections; and to get us to take over some of the burden of supporting Rhodesia.

14. Bishop Muzorewa had resisted this South African pressure. He had told the South Africans that elections were necessary for him to get wider recognition. We had managed to persuade General Walls that the kind of arrangements we had in mind should not affect his relations with South Africa.

15. Mr Botha spoke of the dangers of a Marxist Government emerging

in Rhodesia. The Prime Minister said that a settlement supported only by South Africa and the United Kingdom would leave Rhodesia isolated. It was necessary to offer elections as an alternative to fighting. Lord Carrington said that we must be seen to be reasonable in the conduct of the negotiations. Mr Botha said that Bishop Muzorewa's position should not be weakened. Control of the levers of power was what mattered in African politics. Mr Botha was concerned that Mr Nkomo might contest the elections without accepting the constitution. The Prime Minister said that those participating in the elections would have to do so on the basis of acceptance of the constitution.

16. Mr Botha said that South Africa had a military presence in Rhodesia at Bishop Muzorewa's request. This consisted of equipment rather than men. South Africa was also giving financial support at the rate of some 40 million rand per month. If they were to decide to end their presence, they would wish to do so soon. South Africa could not afford a repetition of what had happened in Angola when they had appeared to capitulate under external pressure.

17. The threat of withdrawal of South African equipment would have rendered it impossible for General Walls to continue to support a settlement. Lord Carrington said that if there were a British presence in Rhodesia during the transition we would not object to South African equipment. General Walls told Mr Botha that he was satisfied with our proposals. The Prime Minister and Lord Carrington were able to use the good offices of Colonel Laurens Van Der Post to continue to keep the South African Government informed, through Dr Koornhof, of our approach. There is no doubt that his efforts, supplementing the regular contacts between our Ambassador in Cape Town and the South African authorities, contributed to South African acceptance of our approach.

18. The Patriotic Front had proposed an interim period of six months, a transitional constitution; a governing Council; a UN peace-keeping force; a UN police force; and the restructuring of the armed forces, police, judiciary and civil service before the elections. We began to explain to African Governments that our ideas were for shorter and much less complex arrangements. The purpose of the pre-independence period was to provide for elections in which all the parties could participate and the people of Rhodesia could choose their future Government. A cease-fire in such a tense military situation was bound to be precarious. A pre-independence period of two to three months should be adequate for elections to be held. In such a period it made no sense to administer the country other than through existing civil service and police. We were committed by the Lusaka agreement to supervising the elections. We were ready to

extend our authority to the administration and the police. President Nyerere continued to insist on a six month transitional period, but President Machel told our Ambassador in Maputo that he agreed that three months should be enough to organise elections.

19. At the same time we explained to other Western Governments that we would be continuing our efforts to carry the Patriotic Front along with us but had to face the possibility that we might not be able to reach agreement with them, while Bishop Muzorewa had accepted the new constitution, fresh elections and the pre-independence arrangement. In such a situation it would be very difficult to withhold independence despite the inevitable damage to our interests elsewhere in Africa.

20. On 17 October in a further bilateral meeting with the Salisbury delegation Lord Carrington explained that the Election Council would be advisory. It would have no executive powers. There would be Commonwealth observers; but they too would not have executive authority. The lifting of sanctions involved a return to legality. This meant the presence of a British administrator or Governor in Rhodesia for a limited period to exercise control through the Rhodesian authorities. This was the only basis on which we could expect to carry our friends with us and assert credibly that the elections we were organising were free and fair. Mr Smith claimed that he had been told that sanctions would be lifted when there was agreement on a constitution. Sir Antony Duff said that an Order in Council appointing a British administrator would provide for existing laws to be carried forward and for the courts and the Commanders to continue in their functions. Lord Carrington acknowledged that if the Patriotic Front refused to participate and accept a cease-fire, there would be difficulties in carrying through this plan; but many of the same considerations would apply. Mr Cronje asked whether it would not be possible to return to the situation under the 1961 Constitution, with a Governor but with the Government still in place. Lord Carrington said that it would not.

21. In the evening the BBC carried the story that we were thinking in terms of a British Governor. Mr Nkomo and Mr Mugabe asked about this when discussing the land question with Lord Carrington on 18 October. They were told that we had not yet come to any definite conclusions.

22. On 19 October, following their acceptance of the independence constitution, discussions on the pre-independence arrangements began with the involvement of the Patriotic Front. Lord Carrington said that an interim period of two months should be sufficient to organise free elections. The registration of voters and the delimitation of constituencies would delay elections by many months.

23. At the same time Sir Antony Duff explained some of our thinking to a team of US officials, who emphasised the US administration's concern

about the black vote and the implications for US interests elsewhere in Africa of the attitude they adopted over Rhodesia. Sir Antony Duff drew attention to the frequently overlooked fact that we were negotiating with two sides, one of which was in possession. Their agreement had to be obtained and we had pushed them a long way. US officials were concerned that, if our arrangements were to be regarded as fair to both sides, Bishop Muzorewa and his Ministers must play no part in the administration of the country. The Americans were told that we were fast approaching a situation in which sanctions were likely to be lifted.

24. On 22 October Lord Carrington told Bishop Muzorewa that any proposal that he should retain responsibility in the pre-election period for the running of the Government could not be defended internationally. Lord Carrington had been confirmed in this view by his discussions with his European colleagues and by talks held with the Americans and French. We could not send the man we had in mind to act as Governor if he was to be a cypher. For a short period responsibility would have to lie with the Governor. Bishop Muzorewa argued strongly that this was unreasonable. If he surrendered executive authority, there would be nothing left to talk about. Lord Carrington said that we had explained to General Walls that there would be no interference with the security forces. If our proposals were not accepted, the patient would die anyway. Bishop Muzorewa did not agree: things might change in time. Lord Carrington said that he was deluding himself. Sir Antony Duff explained that Ministers would not have to make a formal act of resignation. Bishop Muzorewa said that he would have to reflect before announcing his decision.

25. In the Conference on that day Lord Carrington presented our outline proposals for the pre-independence period. These stated that the British Government would be prepared to appoint a Governor, who would have executive and legislative authority. All the political leaders would commit themselves to the election campaign. There would be a British Election Commissioner with supporting staff; and an Election Council. The commanders of the security forces would be responsible to the Governor who would assume authority over the civil police. They would be responsible, under his supervision for the maintenance of law and order. There would be agreement on a cease-fire and the disengagement of the respective forces.

26. On 25 October, at Bishop Muzorewa's request, Lord Carrington held a further bilateral meeting with the Salisbury delegation. He explained that the Governor would need full executive and legislative authority to ensure that the elections were fair. Members of the delegation again expressed their difficulties with the requirement that the Governor should exercise direct control over the administration, police and armed

forces. Lord Carrington said that these powers were essential if the Patriotic Front were to be offered a fair chance of participating in the elections. Mr Ian Smith expressed strong opposition.

27. At a plenary session of the Conference Lord Carrington assured Bishop Muzorewa that all parties participating in the elections must do so on the basis of acceptance of the constitution and must commit themselves to renounce violence and campaign peacefully. The Governor would have to deal with any party that acted outside the law or resorted to intimidation.

28. On 26 October the Patriotic Front tabled further proposals for a UN peace-keeping force, a UN police force and UN supervision of the elections. Lord Carrington said that we were not prepared to accept elements falling outside the Lusaka agreement. It would be for us to supervise the elections; there was no question of UN involvement. Mr Nkomo threatened to appeal to the Commonwealth. Mr Mugabe could not understand why the Conference should consider itself bound by the Lusaka communiqué.

29. On 27 October Bishop Muzorewa announced that his delegation were prepared to accept the broad principles of the interim arrangements, subject to agreement on the practical details. Bishop Muzorewa's agreement that his Government should stand aside was greeted with consternation by the Patriotic Front.

30. On 29 October in bilateral discussions at official level with the Salisbury delegation, we secured agreement on the abolition of censorship during the interim period. Bans on political parties would be lifted as soon as the Patriotic Front accepted a cease-fire. The remaining detainees would be released. Exiles would be permitted to return. Closer to the elections, martial law would be lifted.

31. General Walls was insisting on the need to hold the elections before the end of the year so that, if the Patriotic Front did not agree to a cease-fire, they would be given little opportunity as possible to disrupt them. We were meanwhile intensifying our efforts to persuade Mr Nkomo to accept the proposed interim arrangements and to participate in a settlement. Lord Carrington had a private meeting with him on 30 October. Mr Nkomo continued to insist on a governing council and an international peace-keeping force. He was concerned about his personal safety if he returned to Rhodesia. This meeting was followed up by a series of private meetings between Mr Nkomo and Mr Renwick and Mr Powell.

32. In the Conference the Patriotic Front continued to argue that conditions for free elections could not be established while the existing police were responsible for law and order. Lord Carrington refused to move on to discuss the arrangements for the cease-fire until agreement had been

reached on the interim arrangements. On 1 November he rejected the Patriotic Front's argument that two months would be required for a cease-fire to take effect. On 2 November he tabled our full proposals for the pre-independence period, pointing out that these called for concessions from both sides, but offered the only prospect of ending the war. The proposals stated that the pre-independence period should not be concerned with the remodelling of the institutions of government. This would be a matter for the elected Government. Lord Carrington asked for a response to our proposals at the next meeting of the Conference on 5 November.

33. Commonwealth Governments were told that we did not envisage a peace-keeping force. But there would be provision for the monitoring of the cease-fire under British auspices. Certain Commonwealth countries (Australia, New Zealand, Fiji and Kenya) would be invited to participate in the monitoring process. But we were not prepared to involve countries already committed to the Patriotic Front.

34. On 5 November the Salisbury delegation accepted our detailed proposals. Mr Mugabe replied by raising questions about the judiciary, the armed forces and the civil service. He acknowledged that the independence constitution would allow progressive changes to take place but the Patriotic Front did not want to inherit the existing institutions of the state. On 6 November the Patriotic Front reiterated that these institutions should be 'purged' before the elections took place. The Rhodesian Chief Justice agreed that we might state that in certain circumstances (the election of a Patriotic Front Government) neither he nor his colleagues would wish to continue on the High Court.

35. On 9 November the Patriotic Front put forward further proposals which represented in most respects a re-statement of their paper of 18 September with the important exception that the Governor would be Chairman of the Governing Council, on which there would be equal representation for the Salisbury delegation and the Patriotic Front. On 10 November Lord Carrington replied that it would be for the Governor to conduct the administration in this period: the role of the political leaders would be to put their case to the people of Rhodesia.

36. There had been indications from Lusaka that President Kaunda would welcome an opportunity to see the Prime Minister and, as the moment of decision on the pre-independence arrangements approached, it was decided that this was the time to invite him. He at first seemed withdrawn and unresponsive. The Prime Minister and Lord Carrington explained that there was a serious risk of the Salisbury delegation leaving the Conference if we allowed the Patriotic Front to continue to filibuster.

37. At a further meeting on 10 November the Prime Minister gave President Kaunda a paper outlining our proposals for the cease-fire, including

the establishment of a cease-fire commission and a monitoring force. The paper gave some additional explanations about the arrangements to enable all parties to campaign on an equal footing in the elections; and an assurance that provision would be made for the accommodation and other requirements of the Patriotic Front forces. (This was read into the record of the Conference by Lord Carrington on 14 November). The Prime Minister told President Kaunda that the key to peace was in his hands. We were closer to a solution than ever before, but could only succeed if President Kaunda supported us. Mr Nkomo was showing more interest in an agreement than Mr Mugabe. It would be a tragedy if the latter's intransigence caused the chance to be lost. President Kaunda reacted positively and told Lord Carrington that he was sure that Mr Nkomo wanted a settlement.

38. On 11 November Mr Renwick and Mr Powell held a further meeting with Mr Nkomo, who appeared to realise that decisions could no longer be delayed. He was ready to abandon his arguments for a governing council and about the status of Bishop Muzorewa and to accept that the existing police force should act under the Governor's supervision. He did not object when we said that in certain circumstances the Governor would need to use the Rhodesian security forces. His main concern was with the status of the Patriotic Front's forces. Paragraph 13 of our proposals provided that the Rhodesian forces would be under the authority of the Governor and required to comply with his directions. Mr Nkomo was still probing to see if there was any more give in our position. It was made clear to him that there was not.

39. In a meeting on 12 November Mr Nkomo raised a series of further demands, which were rejected. He appeared, however, to be saying that if we could find a way to meet his anxieties about the status of his forces, he might be able to accept the interim proposals, subject to discussion on the arrangements of the cease-fire. The difficulty in relation to the forces was the acute sensitivity of the Salisbury delegation to any suggestion of 'equality status'. On 13 November Mr Renwick suggested to Mr Nkomo the simple addition to paragraph 13 that: 'The Patriotic Front's forces will also be required to comply with the directions of the Governor'. The Salisbury delegation could hardly refuse to accept such a formulation.

40. On 14 November Lord Carrington insisted on a reply to our proposals. The Salisbury delegation were by this time on the verge of leaving the Conference. Lord Carrington said that, if it was not possible to reach agreement, he would have to report the position to his Cabinet colleagues at 10.30 am on 15 November and ask them to decide our future course of action. He called for a further meeting at 0900 am on the following day.

41. On the morning of 15 November a private conversation took place between Lord Carrington and the Patriotic Front leaders. It was clear the

Mr Nkomo was prepared to agree to our proposals for the pre-independence arrangements subject to the amendment concerning the status of the Patriotic Front's forces. Mr Mugabe was much more reluctant. The Patriotic Front leaders were aware that by this time the enabling Bill had passed both Houses of Parliament and that, if they refused, it was open to the Government to begin to proceed with the internal parties. After a break during which the Patriotic Front leaders conferred together a plenary session was held at 1000 am. Mr Mugabe stated that if the Patriotic Front forces were included in paragraph 13 of the British paper, they could accept the interim proposals, subject to a successful outcome of the negotiations on the cease-fire. Lord Carrington replied that the Patriotic Front's forces, like the Rhodesian security forces, would be required to comply with the directions of the Governor. The necessary amendment would be incorporated in the British paper.

10. Negotiations of the Cease-Fire (November-December 1979)

1. In consultation with the Ministry of Defence, the Department began to work out ideas on the implementation of a cease-fire at the end of September. General Walls had taken a helpful line with Mr Ian Smith (whom he did not like anyway) over the latter's resistance to constitutional change. It was decided that Mr Byatt and Brigadier Reilly should visit Salisbury for confidential discussions with the National Joint Operations Command (NJOC). Their instructions were to impress on the military commanders that in bringing Rhodesia to independence, we must carry other countries with us. We had no intention of putting the Rhodesian forces at a military disadvantage. The elections must be under British supervision. The front-line Presidents were putting pressure on the Patriotic Front to participate. There would need to be a return to legality. If the Patriotic Front did not participate in a settlement, the Rhodesian security forces would have to refrain from cross-border operations. We did not contemplate a large peace-keeping force or UN involvement, though there would be a need for a monitoring force. If the Patriotic Front broke the cease-fire and the police were unable to deal with them, the Rhodesian forces would have to be authorised to assist them. There would need to be a cease-fire commission with Patriotic Front participation. General Walls had repeatedly said that there was no military solution to the war. If we were not able to proceed in this way, we must expect increased Soviet assistance to the Patriotic Front, with the front-line states more strongly committed than ever to support them.

2. On 2 October Mr Byatt reported that the Rhodesian commanders were insisting that the Patriotic Front forces should withdraw to Mozam-

bique and Zambia; or that there should be no cease-fire until after the elections. There were told that such a proposal could not be defended internationally. Their contention was that any form of disengagement which gave the Patriotic Front forces a recognised status within Rhodesia before the elections would be damaging to Bishop Muzorewa and virtually impossible to control militarily. General Walls was adamant that the Rhodesian army must be able to continue normal patrolling during a cease-fire, though they would refrain from offensive operations. A working paper given to the Rhodesians envisaged disengagement on the basis of a concentration by the Patriotic Front forces in pre-determined places within the country. The period of disengagement should not be more than ten days. The Rhodesian forces would discontinue external operations. A cease-fire commission would be established. The Governments of Zambia and Mozambique would be invited to participate in arrangements for the monitoring of cross-border movements. At a further meeting on 3 October the Rhodesian commanders said that they did not believe that a genuine cease-fire could be achieved. The reluctantly accepted, however, that the concept of Patriotic Front withdrawal to designated places within the country merited further examination.

3. The Ministry of Defence began to advance the practical preparations for the contribution we might need to make to the cease-fire arrangements, including a monitoring group, a chairman of the cease-fire commission, and liaison officers with the Rhodesian and Patriotic Front forces.

4. Discussion of the military arrangements was carried forward with General Walls and his colleagues on their arrival in London in mid-October. Sir Antony Duff discussed with General Walls guidelines under which consultations on military matters should take place as necessary between the Governor and the commanders of the defence forces. General Walls wanted Bishop Muzorewa also to be kept informed.

5. The papers on the pre-independence arrangements circulated in the Conference on 22 October stated that there would be agreement between the opposing forces regarding a cease-fire and disengagement of their respective forces. In private discussions, officials continued to impress on General Walls that a credible cease-fire proposal was an essential part of the negotiations and our attempts to win international acceptance. General Wall's agreement was sought to the idea of a monitoring group which would be predominantly British, but which would include Australian, New Zealand, Fijian, and Kenyan representatives.

6. The Government had not hitherto considered sending British forces to Rhodesia. On 27 October the Department noted that no proposals for the regrouping of the forces into zones were likely to be acceptable to either side. The Rhodesians would not accept a UN or Commonwealth

peace-keeping force. We should not be in a defensible position if we were not prepared ourselves to propose arrangements to monitor the cease-fire. Simply to leave responsibility to the commanders on both sides would not be a credible arrangement.

7. On 31 October Mr Lyne wrote to Mr Norbury in the Ministry of Defence about arrangements for the cease-fire. The Governor would need a British military adviser for liaison with the Rhodesian forces. The advisor should be a Major General (the Rhodesian commanders would not accept an officer senior to them). Other senior liaison officers would be required. The object of these arrangements would not be to direct the operations of the Rhodesian security forces, who would be operating within the arrangements agreed for a cease-fire and who would have agreed to cease external operations. General Walls was convinced that some provision for a monitoring group would be a necessary feature of credible proposals for a cease-fire, and that it must be under British auspices. The Australian Prime Minister had indicated that his Government would be ready to consider Australian involvement in tasks additional to election observation as part of a joint Commonwealth effort. The role of the monitoring group would be to observe the cease-fire: in no circumstances would it conduct peace-keeping operations or intervene between the opposing forces. The letter, which was copied to the Prime Minister's office, sought Mr Pym's agreement to the Ministry of Defence proceeding with planning on this basis. On 5 November Mr Norbury replied that a good deal of informal planning had already been done. The monitoring concept discussed with General Walls could be effective but involved considerable difficulties. The monitors would be armed only for personal protection and would have to be withdrawn if the cease-fire broke down.

8. In early November officials sought to refine with General Walls a paper setting out our proposals on the cease-fire in the form in which it would be tabled in the Conference. Following an initial meeting with Lord Soames General Walls again made it clear that he could not accept that the Governor should seek to exercise operational control over the Rhodesian forces. On 15 November General Walls reacted strongly to Patriotic Front claims that, by amending our proposals on the pre-independence arrangements, we had accorded 'equality of status', to the Patriotic Front forces. Lord Carrington said publicly that this had not been the question at issue; what had been at issue was the acceptance by all the forces of the authority of the Governor.

9. On 14 November our posts abroad were instructed to inform the Commonwealth African Governments of the terms of our cease-fire proposals. They were to emphasise that it would be essential to make effective arrangements to monitor cross-border military activity; and to arrange for

the Patriotic Front forces inside Rhodesia to assemble at points where observance of the cease-fire could be monitored. To accept the Patriotic Front's demands that the forces should remain in their existing positions would make an effective cease-fire and the deployment of the monitoring force impossible. This point had been explained by the Prime Minister to President Kaunda and (on the basis of private discussions with Mr Renwick) we believed that it would be accepted by Mr Nkomo.

10. On 16 November Lord Carrington put forward in the Conference our outline proposals for the cease-fire. These envisaged the cease-fire being brought into effect within seven to ten days. The Governments of Zambia, Botswana and Mozambique would be invited to agree on arrangements to ensure compliance with the requirement concerning the cessation of cross-border movement. Britain would take responsibility for the establishment of a cease-fire monitoring group and had invited certain other Commonwealth Governments to contribute to it.

11. For a meeting between General Walls and Lord Soames on 16 November the Department advised that General Walls would require reassurance that he would not be prevented from undertaking patrolling. Command and control of the armed forces would remain in his hands. He would not be required to seek prior authorisation from the Governor for normal activities. But he would be required to consult the Governor on any matters or activities liable to have political implications. It had been made clear to General Walls that it would not be possible for South African units to remain in Rhodesia in the context of a cease-fire. General Walls did not believe that there would be an effective cease-fire. In his view, some of the Patriotic Front forces might assemble but most of them would not do so. We must aim to ensure that in the period during which a cease-fire was brought into effect and the Patriotic Front forces assembled, the Rhodesian forces acted with real restraint. If thereafter Patriotic Front forces were found with weapons in the field, action would have to be taken to deal with this situation.

12. Bishop Muzorewa had decided to return to Salisbury. The Rhodesian commanders were increasingly concerned about infiltration by ZIPRA as the Conference dragged on. Mr Nkomo, who had not previously committed the bulk of his forces inside Rhodesia, was now seeking to do so against the possibility either of his participation in a settlement or to intensify guerrilla activity if we sought to proceed with the internal parties alone. From this point on as the military temperature began to rise the urgency of achieving a settlement became greater than ever.

13. It was clear that the achievement of agreement on the arrangements for the supervision of the forces would be the most difficult element in the

cease-fire discussions. In pursuit of the 'step by step' approach we therefore aimed to seek agreement first on the other elements of our cease-fire proposals, subject to subsequent agreement on the separation of the forces.

14. In the Conference Mr Nkomo argued that the Patriotic Front should have a say in the composition of the monitoring group. On 20 November the Lord Privy Seal replied to the Patriotic Front's cease-fire proposals. It would not be possible to reach agreement on the basis of the allocation of areas to the control of one side or the other. Both sides claimed to be in control of the greater part of the country. Discussions on the demarcation of zones would be prolonged indefinitely. If there was to be an effective cease-fire all the national territory must be under the control of the Governor. We did not accept that it was practicable to envisage a peace-keeping force which would actually enforce the cease-fire. The responsibility for this must rest with the commanders on both sides. He rejected Patriotic Front demands that various units must be disbanded. We did not envisage disbanding any units whether of the Patriotic Front or the Rhodesian forces. Disengagement of the forces would be essential to an effective cease-fire and the deployment of the monitoring group. We envisaged that all Patriotic Front forces inside Rhodesia would assemble during the run down to the cease-fire at places to be decided at the Conference.

15. At a bilateral meeting the British officials including General Farndale, Director of Military Operations in the Ministry of Defence, on 20 November the Patriotic Front delegation, led by General Tongogara, were under instructions to say that they could only discuss the cease-fire arrangement in the presence of the Rhodesian commanders. Attempts by the Patriotic Front leaders to insist on direct military discussions with the Rhodesians were rejected by the Salisbury delegation, who felt that meetings with General Walls would enhance the status of the Patriotic Front commanders and undermine the position of Bishop Muzorewa, with whom the Patriotic Front had refused to negotiate. General Tongogara was obviously attracted, however, by the idea of the cease-fire commission and the role of the Patriotic Front commanders on it. He appeared to understand that a third force, whether it was called a peace-keeping or monitoring force, could not actually enforce a cease-fire. We explained that we genuinely did not believe it possible to achieve agreement on the basis of a demarcation of areas under the control of the two sides.

16. At a plenary session on 22 November Lord Carrington tabled amplified British proposals for a cease-fire. These defined the role of the cease-fire commission and elaborated on the monitoring and liaison arrangements. The activities of the security forces and their maintenance of the cease-fire would be monitored from their existing bases. The Patriotic Front forces inside Rhodesia would assemble at Pre-determined places so

that their maintenance of the cease-fire could be similarly monitored and arrangements made for the security, accommodation and other agreed requirements. Up to fifteen places would be designated for this purpose, with a larger number of intermediate collection points during the assembly process. In the first phase of the cease-fire all cross-border activity would cease and elements of the monitoring force would be despatched to Rhodesia. On cease-fire day all hostilities within Rhodesia would cease. The process of assembly of the forces would begin immediately and should not take more than seven days. Any forces which failed to assemble and to abide by the cease-fire agreement would be acting unlawfully. The primary responsibility for dealing with breaches of the cease-fire would rest with the commanders on both sides through the mechanism of the cease-fire commission and with the assistance of the liaison teams operating with the forces in the regions. In the event of more general or sustained breaches of the cease-fire the Governor would have to decide what action to take to deal with the forces which had accepted his authority. Decisions on post-war military planning would be a matter for the independence Government. The British Government would be ready to assist with the re-settlement of those elements of the forces which wished to pursue a civil career. These proposals were tabled against the background of massive Rhodesian raids into Zambia in response to large scale infiltration by ZIPRA. On 5 November the Rhodesians had suspended maize shipments to Zambia. The Rhodesian raids in the third week of November did halt or impede a considerable amount of movement by ZIPRA towards the Rhodesian border. But they also disrupted completely communications throughout the southern part of Zambia and inflicted heavy damage on the Zambian infrastructure. The Rhodesians also cut rail communications between Zambia and Tanzania. President Kaunda reacted violently to the raids which had been decided by the Rhodesian commanders in Salisbury without reference to General Walls or the delegation in London. The Zambians professed to be convinced the raids had been authorised by us. Demonstrations were organised outside the High Commission in Lusaka. The High Commissioner was recalled to London for consultations. The Prime Minister telephoned President Kaunda in an effort to ensure that this crisis did not result in a withdrawal of his support for a settlement.

17. In the Conference Lord Carrington proposed that the Rhodesians should give an undertaking to carry out no further cross-border operations and that the Patriotic Front leaders should give an undertaking that there would be no further cross-border infiltration. The cooperation of the Zambian authorities would be essential to bring this agreement into effect. This proposal was accepted by Bishop Muzorewa but rejected by the Patriotic Front and the Zambians.

18. The Mozambique Government and some elements of the Patriotic Front (Mr Nkomo and General Tongogara) were by this time showing keen interest in some aspects of our cease-fire proposals. Dealing with the Mozambicans were greatly helped by the fact that President Machel's special representative in London, Mr Fernando Honwana, made clear throughout his determination to help achieve a settlement, if one was attainable. He was conscious of the enormous benefits a settlement would bring to Mozambique. Alone among the front-line representatives, he played an important role in the negotiations. His influence, both with his President and with ZANU, was considerable.

19. On 23 November the Prime Minister issued a statement emphasising that it was essential not to delay agreement on a cease-fire to the point at which previous decisions were imperilled. At the same time it was made clear to the Rhodesian delegation that any further attack on Zambian targets would have serious consequences. The Rhodesians were warned about undertaking a planned attack on the Tete suspension bridge in northern Mozambique. A British military reconnaissance team was sent to Rhodesia to prepare plans for the deployment of the monitoring force.

20. On 23 to 24 November the Patriotic Front leaders attended a meeting with the front-line Presidents in Dar es Salaam. The Zambians did not participate in the meeting and, unusually, no communiqué was issued. President Machel in particular emphasised the importance he attached to a settlement. On their return from Dar es Salaam the Patriotic Front leaders told Lord Carrington on 26 November that they were not yet in a position to reply to our cease-fire proposals. They continued to demand direct discussions with the Rhodesian commanders. Lord Carrington said that unless decisions were taken on the cease-fire there would be a danger of prejudicing all the achievements of the Conference. The Salisbury delegation had agreed that, once agreement was reached on the general framework of our cease-fire proposals, they would be prepared to discuss the practical details of implementation with the involvement of the military commanders.

21. The Patriotic Front failed to attend the plenary session in the afternoon at which the Salisbury delegation accepted its cease-fire proposals. On 27 November in a bilateral meeting Lord Carrington gave the Patriotic Front a detailed explanation of them. The point of main concern was the requirement that their forces must assemble at identifiable places. It was pointed out that the Rhodesian forces were identified and could therefore be monitored. The Patriotic Forces would have to assemble to enable them to be monitored and arrangements made for their security. General Tongogara was concerned about the security of his forces if they assembled and the prospect that the Rhodesian forces would occupy the areas

they had left. Mr Nkomo said that if the Patriotic Front were obliged to move to pre-determined places, the Rhodesian forces must be confined to barracks. Lord Carrington said that the dispositions of the Rhodesian forces would depend on those of the Patriotic Front forces. On 28 November Lord Carrington told Dr Mundawarara that there was no question of the Rhodesian forces being confined to barracks, but we must be in a position to state in the Conference that there would be reciprocal disengagement with the Patriotic Front forces.

22. In the next bilateral meeting Lord Carrington made a statement designed to help the Patriotic Front to accept the cease-fire proposals. This accepted that the monitoring force would need to be larger than had originally been contemplated. It was not practicable to think in terms of any general integration of the forces before independence; but there could be planning for their future in the interim period. The monitoring force would remain in Rhodesia until the independence Government had been formed. The disposition of the forces would depend on the assembly process. On cease-fire day the Rhodesian forces would disengage, enabling the Patriotic Front forces to assemble in secure conditions. They would retain their arms and remain under the authority of their commanders. The process of assembly would take place under the auspices of the monitoring force. A token assembly would not fulfil the obligations of a cease-fire agreement. Lord Carrington had already emphasised that we did not envisage a purge of foreign personnel in the armed forces on either side. But there would be no external intervention in Rhodesia under a British Governor.

23. On 29 November Lord Carrington held a private meeting with the Patriotic Front leaders. Mr Nkomo acknowledged that progress was being made. Mr Mugabe insisted that the Rhodesians must withdraw to barracks. He was not going to permit his forces to be pushed into 'slaughter points'. He was told that the Patriotic Front forces which assembled would be under the protection of the monitoring force. The Patriotic Front leaders said that they would not reply but would pose further question about the disposition of the Rhodesian forces.

24. We concluded that if the Patriotic Front accepted the cease-fire proposals we should have to devise a plan to deal with the otherwise serious danger of indefinitely protracted discussion of the arrangements for implementation. It was decided to make the necessary preparations to enable the constitution to be enacted by Order in Council. At the same time we should be prepared to make the Order in Council concerning the Governor and to effect the return to legality. This would give the Patriotic Front a powerful incentive to agree quickly to the final package. There would cease from their point of view to be any advantage in further delay. In order to make

the final arrangements for the cease-fire we needed a presence in Salisbury. It was decided to introduce the Independence Bill in the House of Commons by 6 December.

25. On 30 November Mr Renwick and Mr Powell saw Mr Nkomo. His objective was to see whether there were any further concessions to be extracted. He complained about Lord Carrington's 'ultimatum'. The meeting ended with Mr Nkomo still taking the line that he could not accept the proposals, though our assessment was that he did intend to accept eventually. Lord Carrington asked the Patriotic Front leaders for their response on 30 November. They produced a paper which proposed that the Rhodesian forces should return to the bases while the Patriotic Front commanders deployed throughout the country. The Rhodesian air force should be grounded. There would be a Commonwealth force reporting to the Commonwealth Secretary General, etc. Lord Carrington rejected these proposals. He said that our proposals were designed to bring about reciprocal disengagement. There would be monitoring arrangements throughout the command structure of the Rhodesian armed forces. Provided the Patriotic Front forces assembled with their arms the disengagement would be complete and reciprocal and neither side would represent a threat to the other. Lord Carrington said that if the Patriotic Front could not accept the cease-fire proposals, subject to discussion of their implementation, it would be impossible to proceed with the work of the Conference.

26. It was by this stage clear that there was considerable pressure within ZAPU to agree to a settlement on this basis. Further discussions with the Patriotic Front took place over the weekend. On 3 December Dr Mundawarara called on Lord Carrington to express his delegation's concern at the continual delays in bringing the Conference to a conclusion. General Walls said that the Salisbury administration were losing ground militarily, with massive infiltration. Lord Carrington gave an assurance that we would not allow the Patriotic Front to exercise a veto over the return to legality.

27. On the same day the Government made the Southern Rhodesia Constitution (Interim Provisions) Order making temporary provision for the Government of Southern Rhodesia by the appointment of a Governor with full executive and legislative authority. Posts were instructed to make clear that this was a further enabling Act. The Order would not come into operation until the Governor was appointed and arrived in Rhodesia and his authority was accepted. The date of the Governor's arrival would depend on developments in the Conference. A primary task would be to normalise Rhodesia's relations with the neighbouring states. The Order enacting the independence Constitution would be made later in the week.

28. Lord Carrington gave a press conference to explain that he had repeatedly asked for a response from the Patriotic Front to the cease-fire proposals we had put forward on 22 November and which had been accepted by the Salisbury delegation on 28 November. He added that we were beginning to take the legislative action to bring a settlement into effect, but in such a way as to leave it open to the Patriotic Front to participate. Our objective remained a comprehensive agreement in which all parties could participate. In private discussions British officials had already agreed with Mr Nkomo a statement that since a number of issues fell within the detailed implementation of a cease-fire the Patriotic Front could accept conditionally the British cease-fire proposals. The Commonwealth Secretary General engaged in consultations with both the Patriotic Front leaders resulting in a statement negotiated by them with Lord Carrington and subsequently read into the record of the Conference on 5 December. This stated that their main concerns were the disposition of the forces, the grounding of the Rhodesian air force and South African forces. Lord Carrington said that there would be no external involvement in Rhodesia under the British Governor. The position had been made clear to all the Governments concerned, including South Africa. The Rhodesian air force would be monitored effectively. Mr Mugabe said that a number of details including the location and number of places for the disposition of the forces fell to be dealt with under the implementation of the cease-fire. His delegation now felt that the British proposals for a cease-fire provided the basis for an agreement and to move on quickly to settle the details of implementation.

29. Lord Carrington emphasised, as he had done in the private discussions, the need to achieve agreement on the implementation of a cease-fire within a very few days and circulated a draft cease-fire agreement. This provided that all the cross-border movement would cease with effect from the day of signature. Provision would be made to permit the return of civilian personnel to Rhodesia. The cease-fire commission would be established under the Governor's military adviser. The British Government would be responsible for the establishment of a monitoring force. On cease-fire day the Rhodesian armed forces would disengage to enable the Patriotic Front forces to begin the process of assembly. The Patriotic Front forces inside Rhodesia would report with their arms to rendezvous positions and thereafter to assembly places. This movement would be completed by cease-fire day plus seven. There would be reciprocal disengagement by the Rhodesian forces in relation to the successful accomplishment of the assembly process by the Patriotic Front forces. Any forces which failed to comply with the cease-fire or with the directives of the Governor would be acting unlawfully. The Governor would decide what action to

take to deal with them with the forces which had accepted his authority. The parties to the agreement undertook to accept the outcome of the elections and to resolve peacefully questions relating to the future composition of the armed forces.

30. The Rhodesians had by this time been pushed into proposing a number of places at which the Patriotic Front forces might assemble within the country. These were all in peripheral areas where guerrilla activity had been intense, which were in close proximity to the frontiers and in which there had been a low turn-out in the 1979 elections. These locations corresponded to General Tongogara's concern to ensure that his forces were not 'encircled' by the Rhodesians. British officials persuaded General Walls to agree to the selection of two or three assembly places in more central areas. Following the selection of fifteen assembly places, associated rendezvous points were chosen to enable Patriotic Front forces to assemble under the auspices of the monitoring force and to be taken to the assembly places. General Walls insisted that the period of disengagement when the Rhodesian forces would be breaking off contact with the guerrillas and standing back from the assembly places and the routes towards them—and thereby relinquishing control—could not be prolonged for more than seven days.

31. On 6 December Lord Carrington told the Conference that our military experts would explain the practical arrangements for the cease-fire at a meeting of experts to be chaired that afternoon by Sir Antony Duff. Both sides must let us know their estimated forces levels inside Rhodesia. The Salisbury delegation made a statement emphasising that a partial cease-fire would not be acceptable. The Rhodesian delegation provided in confidence force levels indicating total forces, including the security force auxiliaries, guard force and reservists of 46,300 men. The Patriotic Front were unwilling at this stage to reveal their force levels. In the afternoon session General Farndale gave the meeting details of the practical arrangements envisaged for the assembly process. The dispositions of the Rhodesian forces would depend on the degree of assembly by the Patriotic Front forces.

32. On the same day Lord Carrington informed the Conference of the contents of the Zimbabwe Bill which would enable Rhodesia to be brought to independence on a date to be decided and made the consequential provisions in United Kingdom law.

33. Preparations were proceeding for the appointment of the Governor. The Prime Minister had decided that, in the event of a comprehensive settlement, the Governor should be Lord Soames. The choice of a senior Cabinet Minister was intended as a further demonstration of the Government's determination to carry the settlement through. Clearly, however, it would

be risky to send a Cabinet Minister to Salisbury in the event of a partial settlement. In that event, it was thought, it might be more appropriate to send a 'professional' Governor. Sir John Paul was provisionally asked to undertake this task. As it became clear that unless we moved quickly to effect the return to legality the chance of a settlement was likely to be lost as a result of a military crisis or the withdrawal of the Salisbury delegation, the Government had to decide whether to risk sending Lord Soames. Lord Soames himself took the view that he should go.

34. On 7 December the Lord Privy Seal announced in Parliament the appointment of Lord Soames as Governor of Rhodesia. Lord Soames would arrive in Salisbury the following week at a date to be decided. The Salisbury Parliament would be dissolved before the Governor's arrival. The presence of a British authority was essential to enable us to bring a cease-fire into effect: otherwise it would not be possible to bring the Rhodesian forces under our control or to make the practical arrangements to enable the Patriotic Front forces to assemble. Without authority in Salisbury we would be unable to prevent cross-border activity or to ensure the resumption of maize supplies to Zambia.

35. The preparations for the return to legality had already been set in hand. From the end of November the advance party of the British military liaison officers under Brigadier Gurdon engaged in consultations with the Rhodesian National Joint Operations Command (NJOC) about the arrangements for the assembly places for the Patriotic Front forces, including logistic support; and the other arrangements for the cease-fire. An advance party from the British Election Commission, in consultation with the Rhodesian National Election Directorate, began to set in hand the preparations for the elections.

36. Meanwhile difficult discussions continued between British officials and General Tongogara and the military experts of the Patriotic Front. The Patriotic Front showed every intention of seeking to prolong the negotiation while they infiltrated more of their forces into Rhodesia. There had been a major movement of ZANLA (Mugabe) forces from Tanzania to Mozambique and ZIPRA (Nkomo) were making repeated attempts to infiltrate large units across the Rhodesia/Zambia border. Against this background, unless agreement on a cease-fire was reached within the next few days, it was unlikely to be achieved at all. If the Governor was not sent to Salisbury the Rhodesians would launch further attacks into Zambia and Mozambique. The purpose of sending him would be to assert our authority and limit these dangers.

37. On 9 December posts abroad were advised that we did not believe it would be possible to delay sending the Governor until the final details were agreed in the Conference. Unless the Patriotic Front were aware that

the return to legality and the lifting of sanctions were actually under way they would have every incentive to continue to filibuster because they believed that it was in their political and military interests to do so. If, however, they were given a strong enough push, we believed that it should be possible to bring them into the settlements. This we intended to do by making the final presentation of our cease-fire proposals to the Conference on 11 December. At the same time we would distribute a map indicating the Patriotic Front Assembly places and the monitoring arrangements for the Rhodesian forces. The return to legality would be effected with the arrival of the Governor in Salisbury and the acceptance of his authority on 12 December. There could be no question of our continuing to apply sanctions against a British Governor: these would be lifted immediately and we should look to our friends and allies to follow suit. Sir Anthony Parsons would be instructed to inform the Security Council. The chances of bringing the Patriotic Front into a settlement would depend in part on the extent of the international support received. If our action was not supported they would be encouraged to hold out and make further demands which would be non-negotiable. If we awaited the outcome of the Conference before sending the Governor it would never come to a conclusion and would be likely to collapse (FCO telegram No 609 to Canberra of 9 December).

38. The Salisbury delegation had by this time agreed to make the necessary dispositions for the dissolution of Parliament and the handing over of executive and legislative authority to the Governor by the morning of 12 December. The final decision concerning the departure of the Governor was not taken until the morning of 11 December. There were very considerable risks involved. We believed by this time that there was a strong possibility that Mr Nkomo at least could be brought to accept our cease-fire proposals. A delay in sending the Governor would have removed the pressure on the Patriotic Front to agree and caused a crisis with the Salisbury delegation, who would have been instructed to return to Rhodesia. The Rhodesians would then have been tempted to see whether parliamentary pressures forced the lifting of the remaining sanctions, while both sides intensified the war.

39. On 11 December the Secretary of State made the final presentation of our cease-fire proposals. Maps were circulated in the Conference setting out the proposed locations of the Patriotic Front's assembly places and the precise arrangements for monitoring the Rhodesian forces. Lord Carrington announced in Parliament that afternoon the departure of Lord Soames for Salisbury. He emphasised that delay would risk prejudicing what had been achieved at the Conference. The Governor's arrival would help to stabilise the situation and normalise relations with the neighbouring coun-

tries. A British authority in Salisbury was necessary to make the final arrangements to bring the cease-fire into effect.

11. The Return to Legality and the Conclusion of the Agreement (December 1979)

1. The Governor arrived in Salisbury at 14:10 hours on 12 December. In the absence of final agreement at Lancaster House it was not possible to seek overflight clearance for the RAF VC10 from Tanzania and Zambia. The flight therefore took place via the Azores and Ascension Island. The Salisbury Parliament had voted unanimously for the return to legality. The Governor was greeted by senior representatives of the armed forces and the civil service. He was accompanied by the Deputy Governor, Sir Antony Duff; the Election Commissioner, Sir John Boynton; and Major-General John Acland, the Governor's Military Adviser, who was also to be the Commander of the Commonwealth Monitoring Force. In a brief statement issued on his arrival the Governor said that he had been asked to hold the government of the country in trust until independence while the political leaders devoted themselves to the election campaign. All parties which wished to participate in the elections should register by 31 December. It was his purpose to work to achieve a secure future for all the people of Rhodesia and to enable it to take its rightful place in the international community. A telegram from Salisbury reported that the Governor had arrived and that his authority had been accepted.

2. In a television address that evening the Governor said that his purpose was to take charge of the administration of Rhodesia for the period necessary to enable elections to be held and for Rhodesia to take its rightful place in the international community. As soon as the elections had been held to decide the new government, he would hand over his powers and the country would become legally independent. This was an irreversible process. All the political parties must be given the opportunity to participate. The Governor would ensure that they would have an equal opportunity to put their case to the people. He would not hesitate to act firmly if anyone sought to subvert the electoral process. The prize of wide international recognition for Rhodesia would depend crucially on the elections. The Governor would be responsible for the administration of the country, working through the public service. It was not his purpose to take decisions or make changes except in so far as they were necessary to enable him to carry out his immediate task. Other issues would be for the independence government to decide. The Governor's task and that of his advisers was to ensure that the administration of the country during the elections was impartial. This would not be an easy period. It was one in which Rhodesia would, he hoped, emerge from a bitter war. The Governor's arrival in

Salisbury was the first step in bringing Rhodesia back to a normal relationship with the rest of the international community. The British Government had that day removed sanctions against Rhodesia and looked to others to do the same.

3. In Washington the State Department spokesman said that the United States welcomed the now complete British proposals for a settlement and urged the Patriotic Front to accept them: President Carter had said that no party should have a veto over fair settlement proposals.

4. Sir Anthony Parsons informed the President of the Security Council that, with the Governor's arrival in Salisbury and the acceptance of his authority, the state of rebellion in the territory had been brought to an end. The situation determined by the Security Council in December 1966 to constitute a threat to international peace and security had accordingly been remedied and the purpose of the measures decided upon by the Council on the basis of that determination had been achieved. In these circumstances the obligations of member states under Article 25 of the UN Charter, in the view of the British Government, were to be regarded as having been discharged. The United Kingdom was terminating the measures (i.e. sanctions) which were taken by it following decisions adopted by the Council in regard to the state of illegality. The African group protested on 14 December against this 'unilateral' action by Britain, arguing that only an affirmative resolution of the Security Council could result in the removal of sanctions.

5. On 13 December Lord Soames had a meeting with Bishop Muzorewa, as a first stage in the take-over of the administration of the country. In the Conference the Salisbury delegation stated that a partial cease-fire would not be acceptable. They doubted whether the Patriotic Front would assemble all their forces. There were also concerned about the continuance of cross-border movement. Subject to satisfactory assurances on these points, they were prepared to sign the cease-fire agreement. Mr Mugabe argued that with the transfer of authority to the Governor the Salisbury delegation had ceased to exist. Mr Nkomo said that the Governor would now be responsible for the conduct of the war.

6. The Patriotic Front continued to argue about the number and location of their assembly places. It was not possible to consider re-negotiating these. Bishop Muzorewa's Government agreed to stand aside on the clear understanding that we would not agree to the siting of Patriotic Front military camps for political purposes. President Machel's reactions to our final proposals had been encouraging. Sir Ian Gilmour told Mr Mugabe and Mr Nkomo that if the Patriotic Front accepted the agreement, the British Government was bound to ensure that it was implemented honourably.

7. The Patriotic Front at last overcame their reluctance to declare their

force levels. They had initially been tempted to declare low figures, in an attempt to reduce the numbers required to assemble. We had made clear that this would not be acceptable. In the military discussions on 13 December they declared their force levels inside Rhodesia as 21,000 for ZANLA and 14,000 for ZIPRA. It was difficult to see how the Patriotic Front could hope to assemble forces of this size.

8. On 14 December Lord Carrington saw Mr Nkomo and Mr Mugabe. They continued to argue for military dispositions which would place them in a more favourable position politically. Lord Carrington said that it was not possible to grant the Patriotic Front bases in areas where they had never been able to establish them by military means. The purpose of the cease-fire agreement was not to grant one side or the other political advantages but to enable elections to be held.

9. By this stage the negotiations turned to a considerable extent on whether it would be possible to produce an extra assembly place for the Patriotic Front in the Midlands. A further assembly point near the Mozambique border, which had been offered by the Rhodesians, would not suffice. The prospects were that in the absence of such an addition, the Patriotic Front would reject agreement on 15 December. ZANU as usual were taking a much harder line than ZAPU. The Governor was told that we were likely to have to say that if the Patriotic Front assembled their forces in numbers greater than the capacity of the existing assembly places, the Governor would have to decide on the action to be taken. The Governor's spokesman made clear that ZAPU and ZANU (Mugabe) would remain banned until they had accepted a cease-fire.

10. Before the final session of the Conference on 15 December Lord Carrington emphasised to Mr Nkomo and Mr Mugabe in a private meeting that what we were talking about was an election campaign not a military campaign. The essential requirement was to achieve an effective separation of the forces. The Patriotic Front political and military leaders would be in Salisbury and the Patriotic Front would be campaigning throughout the country. The political and psychological difficulty for the Salisbury delegation of accepting this (as well as for Bishop Muzorewa in standing aside) was as great as the difficulties the Patriotic Front would face. Mr Mugabe objected that if his forces concentrated they would be at a disadvantage if they had to start fighting again. Mr Nkomo said that he was anxious to have his forces in the political nerve centre of the country.

11. In the concluding session of the Conference Lord Carrington reminded the delegates that agreement had been reached on an independence constitution providing for genuine majority rule, thereby removing the fundamental cause of the war. Rhodesia had returned to legal government

under the authority of a British Governor whose task was to organise elections in which all parties could participate. The Patriotic Front had expressed concern about the number of assembly places allocated to them. Equally strongly felt anxieties had been expressed by the Salisbury delegation as to whether there would be an effective assembly and a cessation of cross-border movement. If the Patriotic Front forces assemble in numbers greater than could be dealt with at the assembly places designated in the cease-fire agreement, the Governor would assess the need for additional sites in relation to the successful accomplishment of the assembly process at places provided for the Patriotic Front forces and to the disposition of their forces. The purpose of our proposals was to offer the parties an alternative to continuing the war. To deny the people of Rhodesia this opportunity to resolve their problems by peaceful means would be unforgivable.

12. Mr Nkomo said that the Patriotic Front could accept the other aspects of the cease-fire agreement but remained concerned about the number and location of the assembly places for their forces. Mr Mugabe, in a very different tone, said that the Patriotic Front's agreement to the independence constitution and pre-independence arrangements had to be conditional. The British Government had demonstrated its partiality throughout the negotiations. The Patriotic Front did not accept our cease-fire proposals and were not bound by any of the agreements reached at the Conference.

13. After the plenary session the Conference Report was initialled by Dr Mundawarara and Lord Carrington. The Report attached the agreements reached on the independence constitution, the pre-independence arrangements and the cease-fire agreement. It stated that in concluding the agreement and signing the Report, the parties undertook:

(*a*) to accept the authority of the Governor;
(*b*) to abide by the independence constitution;
(*c*) to comply with the pre-independence arrangements;
(*d*) to abide by the cease-fire agreement;
(*e*) to campaign peacefully and without intimidation;
(*f*) to renounce the use of force for political ends;
(*g*) to accept the outcome of the elections and to instruct any forces under their authority to do the same.

Dr Mundawarara and the remaining members of the Rhodesian delegation left for Salisbury that day.

14. Despite the deadlock in the Conference it was clear that Mr Nkomo still wanted an agreement; but Mr Mugabe had broken off the negotiations and was preparing to leave for New York to address the United Nations. Sir Antony Duff was asked to impress on the Rhodesian commanders that

it would not be easy to persuade other western countries to follow the British lead in lifting sanctions against Rhodesia unless they were convinced that all reasonable efforts had been made to reach a settlement including the Patriotic Front. It was essential in Rhodesia's interests, but also to carry the Americans and other countries with us, that a final effort should be made to bring in the Patriotic Front, by the offer of an additional assembly place.

15. By 16 December Sir Antony Duff had secured the agreement of the NJOC to the offer of an additional assembly place in the west central area. This offer was passed on to Mr Nkomo and to ZANU. There were by this time reports of President Machel's displeasure at ZANU's attitude in the negotiations. President Machel had told Mr Mugabe that there was no question of 'la luta continua' at Mozambique's expense.

16. At the Prime Minister's request President Carter had already sent messages to the front-line states urging acceptance of our final proposals. The Prime Minister sent a message to the President emphasising that we were very close to agreement in the Conference; and that if the chance of a settlement was to be taken, it was essential that we should get full support. There were divided views in the US Administration, with Ambassador McHenry arguing that the Americans must 'save the British from themselves' and that sanctions should not be lifted without an affirmative resolution in the Security Council. But in response to the Prime Minister's message, President Carter decided that US sanctions against Rhodesia should be lifted at midnight on 16/17 December. This undoubtedly did help to bring home to Mr Nkomo in particular the consequences of a failure to participate in the settlement. Before Mr Mugabe was able to leave for New York, Mr Honwana delivered to him a message from President Machel stating that if he rejected a settlement on these lines he should no longer count on Mozambican support. General Tongogara, who had been engaged in private discussions with Mr Nkomo, was by this time also in favour of concluding the agreement.

17. At 6 p.m. on 17 December the Patriotic Front leaders called on Sir Ian Gilmour (in the Secretary of State's absence in Washington) to initial the cease-fire agreement and the Conference Report.

18. The Governor was informed that it remained difficult to judge how effective an effort the Patriotic Front would make to assemble their forces. The point on which the Patriotic Front were likely to get most sympathy was the time scale for the assembly of their forces. They had agreed to send a first batch of Patriotic Front commanders to arrive in Salisbury on 26 December. Tongogara and Dabengwa both seemed to be disposed to make a serious attempt to assemble their forces and to make the cease-fire work; but it was impossible at this stage to judge with what success.

Tongogara in particular had shown a strong commitment to a settlement. If treated the right way by General Walls and others, he could make a serious contribution to its success.

19. Following the initialling of the agreements the Patriotic Front leaders gave a press conference at which they said that they expected to be allocated additional assembly places. Mr Mugabe said that the assembly process would take six to eight weeks.

20. These statements were reported in the Salisbury *Herald* on the morning of 18 December. They caused a serious crisis in our relations with the Rhodesian military commanders. They had been prepared to offer an additional assembly place in order to bring Mr Nkomo into a settlement. They had not expected or wanted Mr Mugabe's participation.

21. In a meeting between Sir Antony Duff and the Rhodesian military commanders, there was a general feeling of mistrust of our intentions. The Rhodesians sought assurances that the Patriotic Front would have no automatic entitlement to claim additional assembly places; that the seven days allowed for the assembly process would not be extended; that if the Patriotic Front failed to produce the numbers they claimed they should be judged to be in breach of the cease-fire and not be allowed to participate in the elections; and that the Governor would proscribe any political party which broke the cease-fire or the agreement to campaign peacefully. They wanted Lord Carrington in his closing statement to remind the Patriotic Front of what they had undertaken and draw attention to the consequences of non-compliance.

22. Air Marshal McLaren was strongly opposed to the whole agreement. The general feeling of the military commanders was that having made such effort to bring the Patriotic Front into an agreement, we would bend over backwards to keep them in. They did not believe that ZANU had any intention of honouring it; and in that event the British Government would not react.

23. On the advice of the military commanders Bishop Muzorewa wrote to the Governor to say that before he could sign the cease-fire agreement he wanted to see the precise wording of the additions and changes which had reportedly been made to the agreement initialled by Dr Mundawarara. The precise location of the sixteenth assembly place and the principles concerning the requirement for any additional assembly places needed to be clarified. He asked for assurances that press reports that additional assembly places would be opened wherever the Patriotic Front could produce 1,000 men or more were incorrect. A public confirmation was required that all cross-border movement would cease immediately with effect from the signing of the full-cease-fire agreement. An assurance was also required about the numbers of armed men from the Patriotic Front

who would be expected to concentrate in the assembly place, together with a precise time limit for this, in view of Mr Mugabe's reported statement about the time he had in mind for his men to assemble. Bishop Muzorewa also wanted a public confirmation that any failure to concentrate the armed followers of the Patriotic Front in the strengths and time specified in the agreement would be a breach of the cease-fire and would result in the proscription from the elections of the political parties concerned. Cumulative breaches of the cease-fire by any political party should have the same result. At the same time Bishop Muzorewa issued a press statement that he had delayed his return to London to sign the agreements until he had received clarification about the concessions allegedly made by the British Government.

24. The Governor commented that the most difficult point was the Rhodesian wish for an undertaking that he would ban ZANU or ZAPU from participation in the elections in the event of their misconduct; and specifically that we would do this in the event of a failure by the Patriotic Front to assemble their forces in the numbers declared. Once the election campaign had begun, the amount of intimidation and general skulduggery would no doubt increase on both sides. But unless there was an outbreak of fighting clearly amounting to a breakdown of the cease-fire, the Governor found it hard to conceive of circumstances in which it would be politic to ban any party from further participation. If the Patriotic Front failed to assemble most of their forces, the Governor would have to consider the total picture, in particular attitudes and behaviour of those who had not come in. His task therefore was to convince Muzorewa and the Rhodesian military commanders that he would be prepared to impose a ban in certain circumstance, but that those circumstances could not be laid down in advance in any precise terms; and that in any case he would be very reluctant to act in this way. There was, however, a greater possibility of having to proceed against ZANU than against ZAPU.

25. In response to preliminary indications of the NJOC's attitude, the FCO replied that the spokesman had made it clear on the record that there would be sixteen assembly places for the Patriotic Front. The Governor would only consider designating additional sites if the assembly process was so successful that all capacity, including tentage, at the existing sites was exhausted. We did not consider this contingency likely to arise. If it did, no sites would be designated without the agreement of the Rhodesian military commanders. We had made clear to the Patriotic Front that the assembly process must be completed in seven days. Mr Mugabe was saying that it would take much longer. But the seven days were written into the cease-fire agreement. The Patriotic Front were likely, however, to get

considerable sympathy for the view that it might not be practically possible for them to achieve complete assembly of their forces within seven days. But it would be possible by that time to judge how effectively they had tried. If the assembly process clearly had not been effective, there would be a need to take action. If, however, they had made a determined effort to assemble their forces it should be in the Rhodesians' interest to assist the Patriotic Front commanders over the next few days in bringing in Patriotic Forces identified in other areas and to make the assembly process as successful as possible. By beginning the process of normalising relations with Zambia and through the cease-fire arrangements there was a real prospect of de-escalating the war. Although the Rhodesian military commanders did not want this at the expense of political risks, we doubted if this was the prevailing view in the Rhodesian community generally and in particular whether the white community would be prepared for much longer to go on shouldering the existing burden of military service. They would consult the Secretary of State about the possibility of a statement at the signing ceremony emphasising the need for both sides to comply fully with the requirements of the cease-fire agreement.

26. The FCO added that in trying to get over these serious difficulties with the NJOC, the trap which must be avoided was a commitment to ban the Patriotic Front as a whole from participating in the elections if they failed to assemble their forces in the sort of numbers they had declared. There was no difficulty about reassuring the NJOC on the substance of the matter; HMG did not intend to allow the Patriotic Front to win by cheating. But it was essential to proceed in a manner which led them and HMG towards the objective we had defined at the beginning of the process—independence with as wide a measure of international acceptance as possible. The Prime Minister would be willing to see Bishop Muzorewa when he came to London with any NJOC representative he wished to accompany him.

27. Later in the day Sir Antony Duff had a further long discussion with General Walls and Air Marshal McLaren, of which the main feature was their determined effort to obtain an assurance that the Governor would ban the Patriotic Front from participating in the elections if they did not assemble their forces within the seven days. They had convinced themselves that if the Patriotic Front participated in the elections they would win them: the NJOC therefore wished to prevent their participation.

28. In the evening General Walls rang the Head of Rhodesia Department, It was clear that:
   (*a*) General Walls was more or less reassured that we did not envisage more than sixteen assembly places;
   (*b*) He was concerned to get undertakings about the situation which

would arise if the Patriotic Front did not comply with the cease-fire. This would be a *sine qua non* for his agreement and that of Bishop Muzorewa.

29. The FCO noted that in earlier discussions it had been made clear to General Walls that if the Patriotic Front made a serious attempt to assemble their forces, the Rhodesians would have an interest in allowing their commanders, under strict control from the monitoring force, to help bring in additional elements in the countryside. Lord Carrington had said in the Conference that a token assembly would not be sufficient. But the Patriotic Front could not be disqualified on the basis of a failure fully to assemble the unrealistic totals they had declared if they were in fact making a serious attempt to assemble. If there was a derisory assembly by ZANLA, the Governor might have to take action vis-à-vis ZANU after the end of the assembly process, though this would have to be preceded by repeated warnings to them.

30. That evening the Governor was authorised to deliver the Prime Minister's reply to Bishop Muzorewa. This gave an assurance that the only difference between the agreement initialled by Dr Mundawarara on 15 December and that initialled by the Patriotic Front on 17 December was the addition of one extra assembly place for the Patriotic Front forces. The cease-fire agreement required the cessation of all cross-border movement from midnight on the day of signature. The cease-fire would come into effect seven days after signature of the agreement. The Patriotic Front would be expected to complete the assembly of their forces within seven days after that. Any forces which had not assembled after that date would be unlawful and in breach of the cease-fire agreement. In signing the Conference Report all parties had entered into binding commitments. These would be emphasised again at the signature ceremony. The Governor would have to take whatever action was necessary to deal with the situation in which any party failed to comply with the obligation to campaign peacefully and the cease-fire. The Prime Minister expressed her belief that the settlement which Bishop Muzorewa had done so much to make possible would provide a secure future for his country. The Prime Minister looked forward to seeing Bishop Muzorewa to discuss these and any other concerns.

31. In passing on the Prime Minister's message to Bishop Muzorewa, Lord Soames said that what action he would take in relation to Patriotic Front forces which failed to assemble within the prescribed seven days would depend on his judgement of the total situation, including the numbers who had not reported and their behaviour. He could not give any precise undertaking as to what he might think it necessary to do in any given circumstances. But he had plenary powers and would have to take action

against any political party which systematically broke the cease-fire and its connected commitments to campaign peacefully and without intimidation. He would regard very seriously a failure to make any real attempt to comply with the assembly process. Bishop Muzorewa agreed to attend the signature ceremony in London on 21 December.

32. General Walls and Mr Flower (Director of the Rhodesian Central Intelligence Organisation) arrived in London on the evening of 20 December (the day before the signature ceremony). In discussion with the Head of Rhodesia Department General Walls agreed to the time-scale for the cease-fire. The provision concerning cross-border movement would come into effect at midnight on 21 December. All hostilities would cease at midnight on 28/29 December. The assembly process would be completed at midnight on 4/5 January.

33. The Rhodesians maintained their refusal to sign the agreements unless the consequences of a failure to honour them were made clear in a closing statement to the Conference. Particularly in view of Patriotic Front statements that it might take weeks to bring the ceasefire into effect, we considered this to be desirable in any event, in order to exert maximum pressure in favour of compliance. Bishop Muzorewa was told that Lord Carrington would state that no party could expect to take part in elections if it continued the war or systematically to break the cease-fire.

34. At mid-day on 21 December, at the ceremony at Lancaster House attended by the Prime Minister, the leading members of the British, Salisbury and Patriotic Front delegations, the Commonwealth High Commissioners and other members of the diplomatic corps, the signature of the final report of the Lancaster House Conference was preceded by a speech by Lord Carrington. Lord Carrington congratulated the participants in the Conference on its successful outcome. This was of the greatest significance to the people of Rhodesia and the neighbouring states. The people of Rhodesia would now be able to settle their future by peaceful means. In signing the documents, the delegations had now pledged themselves to certain solemn undertakings. The British Government intended faithfully to discharge the heavy responsibilities it had undertaken. It was essential to the success of the enterprise that all the parties should realise that what had been signed at the conclusion of the Conference were solemn and binding agreements. It would be for the Governor to see that the parties acted in accordance with these commitments. The moment for which the people of Rhodesia had been waiting would come at midnight on 28 December. At that time all hostilities within Rhodesia would cease. The successful accomplishment of the disengagement and assembly process would be of crucial importance to the successful completion of the cease-fire. The subsequent commitments concerning the political campaign by

peaceful means were of no less importance. Lord Carrington added: 'Our commitment is to fair elections. Having committed themselves to campaign peacefully and to comply with the cease-fire agreement, no party or group could expect to take part in elections if it continued the war or systematically to break the cease-fire and to practice widespread intimidation'. In accepting these commitments, the parties had given the people of Rhodesia new hope for the future. At the end of a bitter conflict lay the prospect of national reconciliation. In concluding the Conference, he thanked both delegations for reminding the world, at a time when it was very much in need of it, that there was a genuine alternative to conflict.

Colleagues and friends at Government House. Seated from left: Nicholas Fenn (FCO), James Buckley (Civil Service Dept.), Col. Andrew Parker Bowles, Lady de Rothschild, Lord Soames, Lady Soames, Sir Evelyn de Rothschild, Sir Antony Duff (FCO).

Lady Soames with children.

Popular Front fighters at an assembly area.

The Zimbabwe Independence State Banquet: Robert Mugabe, Lord Soames, Lord Carrington.

The Zimbabwe Independence State Banquet: HRH The Prince of Wales, Robert Mugabe, Joshua Nkomo, Lord Carrington (Cecil Rhodes looking on).

The Zimbabwe Independence State Banquet: HRH The Prince of Wales, Robert Mugabe, Lord Soames, Lord Carrington.

PART II

THE RHODESIA SETTLEMENT: THE GOVERNOR'S ADMINISTRATION IN
SALISBURY
(DECEMBER 1979—APRIL 1980)

PERSONAL COMMENTARY

1. The attached account of the Governor's administration in Rhodesia
deals with the main political and military problems and only cursorily with
other aspects of Lord Soames' administration, including the return of a
large number of refugees, the re-opening of the frontiers, the normalisation
of the country's economic relations with the rest of the world; and the in-
defatigable work of Lady Soames on behalf of charitable organisations and
the refugees. A full account of the work of the Election Commission has
already been given by Sir John Boynton.

2. As will be clear from these papers, the Governor encountered great
difficulties, especially in the early part of his administration. The situation
in the country was extremely tense. The danger of a breakdown of the
cease-fire was ever-present. Many white Rhodesians, including elements
of the armed forces, were far from being reconciled to the changes which
were taking place. The Patriotic Front were no less suspicious of our intentions. The hostility between the two sides, who had been engaged in a
war in which the worst atrocities had been committed, was intense. The
Governor and his staff were not in a position to impose their wishes on the
Rhodesian administration. It was necessary to proceed by a process of continual negotiation. This imposed a considerable strain on the resources of
Government House and on all concerned. But it was inevitable in the process of putting a settlement into effect. The difficult task of administering
Rhodesia took place against the background of a fine display of international hypocrisy, culminating in President Nyerere's announcement on the
eve of the poll that he would only accept the result if the Patriotic Front
won.

3. The Rhodesian military commanders were never really reconciled to
the participation of ZANU and spent much of their time trying to get them
excluded from the elections. The full extent of South African military involvement only became apparent after the Governor's arrival in Rhodesia;
and this too caused the most serious concern until agreement was reached
at Sir Antony Duff's meeting with Mr P.W. Botha on 26 January. There
was intimidation in the eastern provinces; ZANU were preventing other

parties from campaigning in them. It was necessary to exert continual pressure on them to comply with the agreements if we were to get through to the elections at all. As ZANU feared that they might be banned in certain areas and the press and other observers were encouraged to visit them, there was an improvement in the situation in the three weeks before the election.

4. But ZANLA misconduct was only part of the story. There was a series of violent attacks on leading members of ZANU, culminating in an attempt to assassinate Mr Mugabe which failed only narrowly on 10 February. The 'psychological operations' branch of the Rhodesian forces continue to pour out politically inept and embarrassing propaganda. Two members of the Selous Scouts blew themselves up in an attempt to attribute to ZANU responsibility for the bombing of churches in Salisbury.

5. In the run-up to the elections, the Governor had to consider whether some action should be taken to penalise ZANU, e.g. by postponing the elections in the areas worst affected by intimidation. The Governor had no doubt that it was best to avoid such a step. It would have been used by ZANU and by a host of external critics to seek to invalidate the elections while making no difference to the overall result. The difficulty was in bringing the Rhodesian commanders to accept this and ensuring that they did not precipitate a breakdown of the cease-fire. Matters came to a head on the eve of the elections, but General Walls rejected Mr Ian Smith's arguments for denunciation of the Lancaster House agreement and told Bishop Muzorewa that it was best to proceed. In the event the size of the ZANU victory could not possibly be explained by intimidation. Virtually the entire Shona-speaking population voted for them.

6. The next task was to ensure that the Rhodesian commanders accepted the result; and that Mr Mugabe saw the need to accommodate Mr Nkomo and ZIPRA, and the Rhodesian forces and the white community, if the authority of his government was to be consolidated. The fact that the transition to independence was a smooth and orderly one was due above all to the personal relationship the Governor established with him. On all major issues Mr Mugabe sought and valued the Governor's advice and acted on it in his public statements, the formation of his government and the establishment of the joint military high command. There could be no greater tribute to Lord Soames than that the two sides who had been so critical and suspicious of Britain in the period preceding the elections united thereafter in urging him to prolong his role.

7. Relations with General Walls were difficult throughout. With the failure of Mr Ian Smith, he felt himself responsible for the future of the white community and of Rhodesia. He was under constant pressure from

the Rhodesian Front and from elements of his own forces. It was in personal terms extremely painful for him to find himself cast among the white community as a 'sell-out'. It was difficult at times exhausting business to seek to ensure that he and his colleagues took the right decisions. But, with the encouragement of Mr Flower and Mr David Young, at the crucial stages he did take the right decisions while continuing at times to protest that he had been 'let down'.

8. Against most expectations, it was in the end possible to ensure that Rhodesia did not go the way of Algeria and that the final convulsions of a war in which 20,000 people had been killed were avoided. After the history of the last fifteen years the country faces enormous problems. It can hardly be expected to escape many of the difficulties which have beset other African countries. But Rhodesia was brought to independence in circumstances incomparably better than could have been imagined a year ago. Despite the political blindness of the Rhodesian Front, race relations in Rhodesia never seemed irredeemable. White and black Rhodesians did not detest each other in personal terms, Tongogara found no difficulty in talking with Mr Ian Smith. This contributed greatly to the attempt to set the country on a different course. In his independence message Mr Mugabe paid tribute to Lord Soames for the way in which he had guided the country to independence. 'It was from the outset a most difficult and unenviable task.'

24 July 1980   R.W. RENWICK

THE RHODESIA SETTLEMENT: THE GOVERNOR'S ADMINISTRATION IN
SALISBURY

1. The Implementation of the Cease-Fire (December-January 1980)

1. The Governor arrived in Salisbury on 12 December. The Salisbury
Parliament had voted unanimously for the return to legality. The Governor
was greeted by senior representatives of the armed forces and the civil
service. He was accompanied by the Deputy Governor, Sir Antony Duff;
the Election Commissioner, Sir John Boynton, and Major-General Acland,
the Governor's military advisor, who was also to be the Commander of the
Commonwealth Monitoring Force. The police band played 'God Save The
Queen'. Among the crowds outside Government House was Sir Humphrey
Gibbs, who was one of the first to call on the Governor. At Government
House the Union Jack was raised. The Governor said that his task was to
hold the government of the country in trust until independence while the
political leaders devoted themselves to the election campaign. Wide international recognition would depend on the elections, in which all political
parties must be given the opportunity to participate. 'For a war-weary
country the prize is great'. With the return to legality the British Government had that day raised sanctions against Rhodesia and looked to others
to do the same.

2. On the following day Lord Soames had a meeting with Bishop Muzorewa as the first step in the takeover of administration of the country.
Over the next few days he saw the other outgoing Ministers, the permanent
secretaries and the Police Commissioner. Mr Ian Smith had many reservations about the Lancaster House agreement 'but there was no turning back
now'. In public he said that Rhodesia was going through the darkest period
in its history, having been compelled for the first time to 'hand over control
to outsiders'.

3. The Governor began the process of normalising relations with the
neighbouring countries by ordering the resumption of maize supplies to
Zambia. Planning began for the return of the refugees from Botswana,
Zambia and Mozambique. General Acland reported astonishment among
the Rhodesians that the monitoring force should be prepared to take on a
task so fraught with hazards in the rendezvous points and assembly areas.
The planned deployment did everything possible to reduce the risks. We
would, however, be on a knife edge from cease-fire day, when the monitoring teams were left on their own in widely dispersed areas awaiting the
arrival of the Patriotic Front forces, until the assembly process was completed.

4. The early days of the Governor's administration were dominated by
the crisis with the Rhodesian military commanders over the conclusion of

the Lancaster House agreement. They were never really reconciled to the participation of ZANU (Mugabe) in the settlement. They did not believe that ZANU would honour the Lancaster House agreement and feared that their participation would affect Bishop Muzorewa's electoral chances. Lord Carrington had warned that no party could expect to participate in the elections if it continued the war and systematically broke the ceasefire. This was designed to exert pressure on the Patriotic Front to comply with the agreement. Our attitude was bound to depend to a considerable extent on whether or not both wings of the Patriotic Front made a serious attempt to assemble their forces.

5. The difficulties the Governor was to experience with white opinion in Rhodesia were demonstrated from the outset, when his decision to exercise the prerogative of mercy by commuting the death sentences in eleven cases of murder provoked an outcry in the press and on the part of Rhodesian Front politicians.

6. The question of South African involvement also posed serious problems. Lord Carrington had stated in the Conference that there would be no external intervention in Rhodesia under the Governor, but that we would not be seeking to organise a purge of foreign or other personnel in the Rhodesian forces or in those of the Patriotic Front. Lord Carrington made it clear to General Walls in London that it would be impossible for us to accept the presence of South African units in Rhodesia under a British Governor. The South African Ambassador in London was told that there must be no formed South African units in Rhodesia under the Governor; and this was confirmed by Mr Leahy to Mr Pik Botha. The full extent of South African involvement was discovered only after the Governor's arrival. Lord Soames reported on 20 December that a Rhodesian company had taken over from the South Africans patrolling forward from Beitbridge; but that some South African elements remained at Beitbridge. The Governor thought that a respectable case could be made for permitting South Africans to be on Rhodesian soil for the sole purpose of protecting the bridge, which was vital to both countries and to Zambia. It was better to come clean over this.

7. Apart from the contingent at Beitbridge, there were three other companies composed almost entirely of South African personnel in the south east area, as well as some helicopters with their crews and some fixed wing aircraft. General Walls insisted that these were essential to Rhodesian security. Lord Carrington agreed that a statement should be made about Beitbridge; but the position thereafter would depend on how effective the cease-fire was. General Walls and the South Africans had been told that we would not require the withdrawal of South African personnel provided they were integrated in the Rhodesian forces; but there must be no regular

or formed South African units. General Walls should be told that we did not accept his interpretation of what had been agreed. If South African personnel were retained, they must be fully integrated into the Rhodesian forces. If the position became known we should have no alternative but to insist on withdrawal.

8. On 21 December, the day of the signature of the Lancaster House agreement, the Governor lifted the bans on ZAPU (Nkomo) and ZANU (Mugabe) and granted a general amnesty concerning political acts done in good faith whether in furtherance of or in opposition to the illegal declaration of independence. The first transport aircraft carrying British troops and equipment began to arrive in Salisbury. Britain provided 850 out of the 1,200 men in the Commonwealth monitoring force. On 26 December the first group of Patriotic Front commanders arrived and were greeted by a large crowd at Salisbury airport. The Patriotic Front military headquarters was established at the University. At our request Mr Nkomo had already made a broadcast giving clear instructions to his forces to cease fire and report to the assembly places. Mr Mugabe's broadcast from Maputo suggested that British imperialism would be trying to run in the elections 'under cover of the puppet Muzorewa'. On the same day news arrived of the death of Tongogara in a car accident in Mozambique.

9. On 29 December the Governor reported that the first day of ceasefire had been marked by the successful deployment in extremely difficult conditions of the monitoring force. A modest number of Patriotic Front personnel had appeared with their arms. Some who had made contact with the monitoring teams and the Patriotic Front liaison officers had gone back again into the countryside to bring in larger groups. There were preliminary indications of movement by ZANLA across the Mozambique border and a potentially serious confrontation between Rhodesian forces and ZANLA at a protected village on the border. On the following days there were further reports of cross-border movement by ZANLA. Rhodesian action against ZANLA forces refusing to move in the Bindura area was narrowly avoided by prompt action by the monitoring force. The Mozambican military authorities, with whom contact was established near Umtali, said that it was very difficult for them to control cross-border movement.

10. The Governor made clear that there was no question of extending the assembly period, which was part of the Lancaster House agreement. ZANLA were exploiting the disengagement of the Rhodesian forces by organising 'victory marches'. It was essential to maintain the pressure on the Patriotic Front forces to assemble on time. But arrangements were worked out with the Rhodesian commanders to allow movement from the rendezvous points to the assembly places on the day after the formal ending of the assembly process. By this time cross-border liaison had been

established with Zambia as well as Mozambique. Mr Fernando Honwana arrived in Salisbury as the representative of President Machel.

11. By the afternoon of 4 January 9,000 Patriotic Front personnel had assembled. The Patriotic Front military commanders broadcast last minute appeals to their men to assemble. The commitment to make the cease-fire work seemed much stronger on the ZIPRA side. The Governor reported that when the assembly process had been completed he would authorise the Rhodesian forces to assist the police in dealing with armed groups which had no intention of complying with the cease-fire and which had rejected further appeals to assemble. The Rhodesian forces had already been deployed to check cross-border movements. But we would be trying to use the Patriotic Front military commanders to bring in 'outstanding' groups. The Governor would have to take firm action to demonstrate that he was not prepared to accept breaches of the cease-fire, systematic intimidation or incitement to violence; otherwise the situation would quickly get out of control.

12. By 5 January the Patriotic Front had assembled over 15,000 men. There was a de facto extension of the assembly process throughout 5 and 6 January. Once this process had been completed other Patriotic Front personnel wishing to join the assembly process were normally required to do so without their arms, which were in normal cases handed over to the monitoring force. In the evening the Governor reported that in the last phase of the assembly process there had been a massive influx of Patriotic Front forces—nearly 10,000—in the last thirty-six hours. There had been a sudden very large increase in the camps near the eastern border with Mozambique. But there clearly had been a major effort by the Patriotic Front commanders to assemble their forces. The Rhodesian authorities had cooperated in extending the assembly period. This was a very satisfactory outcome for which great credit was due to the monitoring force. The last minute influx had borne out the need to adhere to the deadline specified in the Lancaster House agreement, while in practice seeking to apply it with some flexibility. It would reduce the serious problems which had developed throughout Rhodesia as the Patriotic Front forces attempted to take maximum political advantage of the assembly period before moving to assembly places. There were still large armed bands in the countryside. Some of these owed allegiance to ZANLA; others were engaged in banditry. There appeared to have been a near-complete assembly of the ZIPRA forces. There would be a period of very considerable tension over the next few days. But the results so far had exceeded all expectations.

13. The attitude of the white community towards Mr Nkomo was still dominated by the reactions to the shooting down by ZIPRA of two civil aircraft and the massacre of the survivors from one of them. There were

fears about his safety when he returned to Rhodesia; at his request he was provided with British police protection. Before leaving London Mr Nkomo made a series of statements about the need for national reconciliation. This was to be his theme throughout his campaign. ZIPRA had demonstrated by their conduct during the assembly process a commitment to make the cease-fire work. An advance group of ZAPU officials had been in Salisbury for some time. Mr Nkomo had planned to return on 6 January, but a rally held by Bishop Muzorewa in Salisbury on that day would have caused a danger of clashes between their supporters. Mr Nkomo agreed to return and address his rally on the following Sunday, 13 January.

14. There were by this time over 20,000 Patriotic Front personnel in the assembly places. Under constant pressure from the monitoring force and the Governor's staff, the Rhodesian forces continued to act with restraint. After the end of the assembly process they were required on several occasions to deal with recalcitrant ZANLA groups. In all such cases the problems were resolved, usually by the rapid intervention of the monitoring force, sometimes after tense and difficult negotiations.

15. As the 'outstanding' groups became smaller in size and more recalcitrant it was not possible to deploy the monitoring force or Patriotic Front liaison officers in every case. On 10 January in an incident at Lupane the police opened fire and seven ZIPRA personnel were killed. This provoked an outburst from President Nyerere and, to a lesser extent from Mr Nkomo. The Lupane incident was exceptional: the police had in general been doing their utmost to resolve such incidents peacefully. There were by now nearly 6,000 ZANLA personnel in assembly place Foxtrot alone. Movement in and out of this camp was to cause difficulties throughout the period up to the elections. There was evidence that ZANLA commanders have given instructions that a portion of their forces should remain outside the assembly areas. There were incidents of villagers having been told that unless they voted for ZANU the war would continue and they would be killed.

16. The Patriotic Front commanders were used whenever possible to deal with breaches of the cease-fire. It was not possible to agree to their demands that their forces should be used. The Rhodesians would not accept this; and in a precarious cease-fire it would have been extremely hazardous to invite the Patriotic Front forces to come out of the assembly places. In the nine days after the formal end of the assembly process a further 2-3,000 men were 'talked in' while the Rhodesian forces were kept out of the way. From mid-January the flow was very much reduced and the groups still outstanding were clearly determined not to assemble.

17. Mr Nkomo returned on 13 January and was taken in a monitoring

force helicopter to address a political rally attended by 120,000 people. By this time the cease-fire was holding reasonably well and the level of violence had fallen substantially. Many of the incidents reported, including stock theft, appeared to be criminal rather that political. But the Rhodesian commanders insisted on continuing to issue daily communiqués deliberately exaggerating these incidents and ignoring the enormous improvements in the situation throughout the country since the cease-fire came into effect. The communiqués were politically inept and embarrassing. They also began to try to build up a dossier of evidence much of it genuine but all of it presented in an exaggerated manner of ZANLA misconduct to support the demands for the exclusion of ZANU from the elections.

18. By this time it was clear that Mr Nkomo's hopes that the two wings of the Patriotic Front would be obliged by the front-line Presidents to fight the elections as a single party (with himself in the leading position) had finally been disappointed. Mr Nkomo's reluctance to break with Mr Mugabe at Lancaster House was not shared by ZANU once the Conference was over. They regarded Mr Nkomo as a tribal leader and had no doubt that they would win a far higher proportion of the votes of the Shona-speaking population (80% of the electorate) without him.

19. In the regular meetings held by Sir A. Duff with the National Joint Operations Command (NJOC) we attempted to get the Rhodesian commanders to plan more seriously for the future of the Patriotic Front forces in the assembly places. The Patriotic Front commanders accepted that a proportion of their forces would have to return to civilian life; but naturally insisted in knowing first how many would be accepted in the future army. General Walls and Mr Flower showed an understanding of the need to plan for the integration of the forces. But all attempts to devise plans for this foundered for several weeks on the obtuseness of the Rhodesian commanders.

20. The atmosphere in the assembly places varied from the friendly to the tense. The Rhodesians began to allege that there was movement on a large scale in and out of the assembly places, that local people were being brought to them to attend political meetings and that a high proportion of those who had reported were not guerrillas but youthful 'mujibas'. The Rhodesian reports exaggerated the difficulties, but there was a good deal of movement in and out of the assembly area. The cease-fire commission attributed the great majority of confirmed breaches of the cease-fire to ZANLA or ZANLA operational areas.

21. Immediately after the completion of the assembly process, the Governor's spokesman had stated that South African forces were present, with the Governor's agreement, at Beitbridge for the sole purpose of helping to

assure the protection of the bridge, which was the essential communications link between South Africa, Rhodesia and Zambia. This provoked an international outcry and Lord Carrington and the Governor remained deeply concerned about the problem. General Walls was concerned about the potential threat posed by the large number of Patriotic Front forces in the assembly places. His objective was to keep the South Africans involved in the defence of Rhodesia.

22. By this time we were heading for a second crisis in our relations with the Rhodesian commanders. On 8 January the Governor reported that the whites feared that if the elections brought ZANU into power, they would not abide by the constitution. There would be trials and purges and no future for the white community. They were not in a mood to resign themselves to a Patriotic Front Government. Their fears were shared by many of ZANU's African opponents. The Rhodesian Front would win all the white seats but were themselves divided, with Mr David Smith and the moderates supporting Bishop Muzorewa and Mr Ian Smith flirting with Mr Nkomo. The Rhodesian military commanders were exercised about the behaviour of ZANLA during the assembly process and of ZANLA groups since it had ended, as well as by the extent of cross-border movement. The main immediate problem would be in dealing with the persistent and co-ordinated pressure from the military commanders, the police, the administration and Bishop Muzorewa to exclude ZANU from the elections in view of the conduct of ZANLA. Action against ZANU was not a step which should be taken except in the last resort and not in any event before we had tied Mr Nkomo and ZAPU firmly into the electoral process.

23. The only existing powers available to the Governor were to ban a party as a whole from participating in the elections. This, we had no intention doing. To exert maximum pressure on all the parties to comply with the agreements, to contain the tense and difficult situation which would prevail over the next few weeks and to deal with the general problem of intimidation, the Governor intended to make an Ordinance stipulating that if any electoral district serious breaches of the agreement were consistently committed by the supporters of a political party, he might declare that party to be disqualified from contesting the elections in the district concerned. Banning a party in any electoral district would provoke a very sharp reaction, but the promulgation of the Ordinance should in itself exert a pressure on all the parties to comply with the agreements. It might be necessary to make use of the powers under this Ordinance if the situation continued to be as disturbed as it had been in the eastern districts.

24. On 10 January the Governor reported that at a meeting of the National Security Council the Rhodesian commanders and the Police Commissioner argued that there was no commitment on ZANU's part to make

the cease-fire work. Instructions had been sent to ZANLA not to assemble all their forces and to infiltrate as many personnel as possible from Mozambique. ZIPRA were making a serious effort to comply but ZANU had deliberately left enough ZANLA cadres in the villages to maintain their capacity for intimidation. The police had discovered ZANLA arms caches and were arranging for the Governor's police advisers to interview captured ZANLA personnel.

25. The Governor accepted that there was *prima facie* evidence of deliberate evasion by ZANLA of obligations under the cease-fire agreement. But he did not believe that it would be right to 'excommunicate' ZANU. He told the Rhodesian commanders that he would be taking powers to make a graduated response to any party systematically breaching the cease-fire or other agreements. He did not know whether or when the moment would come to use these powers. If he was to consider action against any party, this must be based on firm evidence. It was essential to lock Mr Nkomo into the electoral process and not to ruin the prospect of normalising relations with Mozambique. We had to have regard to the international reactions: we wanted the elections to win international acceptance. General Walls accepted the need to bring in Mr Nkomo, but argued that cross-border movement by ZANLA and the instructions to ZANLA cadres to stay outside the assembly places and exert pressure on the local population were violations of the Lancaster House agreements. The Rhodesians had been assured that we would not permit a party to win the elections by these means. The Governor said that the NJOC should not under-estimate the difficulties for him in taking action against a party. He would have to be able to present an indisputable case to world opinion. If such action were to be taken, the conduct of others must be above reproach—including the security force auxiliaries. In reporting on the meeting the Governor commented that, while concerned about intimidation, the Rhodesian commanders clearly also were concerned about ZANLA's capacity to win the elections in any event.

26. Lord Carrington endorsed the line taken by the Governor. The assembly process and cease-fire had been more successful than anticipated. International opinion was not at all prepared for such drastic action as the banning of ZANU. In that event ZANLA forces would leave the assembly places and resume the war in circumstances in which President Machel would have no option but to support them. The British Government would wish to think long and hard before accepting responsibility for a war as well as an election. The evidence of ZANLA misbehaviour, though disturbing, had not yet reached proportions where it could be considered a sufficient basis for action against the political wing. The Governor was right not to raise Rhodesian expectations of such action, while leaving the

way open for piecemeal measures against well-documented ZANU infractions.

27. On 12 January President Nyerere held a press conference to criticise our actions in Rhodesia and threatened to break off diplomatic relations. On 15 January the Governor's spokesman drew attention to the achievements of the Governor's administration since his arrival. Over 21,000 Patriotic Front personnel had assembled. Cross-border liaison had been established with Mozambique, Zambia and Botswana. There had been a decrease in the number of incidents throughout the country. Maize shipments had been resumed to Zambia. Border crossing points had been opened. Air services were being resumed. Most western governments had opened or were opening offices in Salisbury. A conference had been held in London on 4 January with the representatives of the UNHCR, ICRC, the front-line States and the Patriotic Front to set in hand preparations for the return of refugees, beginning later in the month. Most censorship provisions had been lifted and bans on publications removed. Prohibited immigrants were being re-admitted. A general political amnesty had been declared. The great majority of people detained under emergency powers had been released. Martial law courts had been suspended. The number of martial law detainees was being reduced. Preparations were in hand for the elections. Leading members of both wings of the Patriotic Front had returned or were returning to Rhodesia. There would be equal access to the media for all parties. The Governor had addressed the first meeting of the Election Council. Sanctions had been lifted. We were close to agreement on preferential access for Rhodesian exports to the European Community. On the following day the European Community agreed to grant duty-free access for the majority of Rhodesia's exports.

2. The Approach to the Elections (January-February 1980)

1. In the period during and following the assembly of the Patriotic Forces it had been possible to persuade the Rhodesian forces and the police to act sensibly and with restraint in virtually all the difficult and dangerous confrontations which had taken place with elements of the Patriotic Front forces. But the cease-fire remained fragile and was liable to break down if there was precipitate action by either side. Relations with the military commanders remained very difficult. They were moving towards the conviction that it might be necessary to come to terms with Mr Nkomo; and we continued to push them towards making a start with the integration at least of some ZIPRA elements before the elections took place. But the situation was liable to get out of hand if ZANU were permitted to get away with manifest breaches of the agreements. It was made clear to ZANU by HM Ambassador in Maputo and through the Mozambicans that we required

firm undertakings about the release and return to Rhodesia of ZANU dissidents held in Mozambique before Mr Mugabe returned to Salisbury.

2. By the third week of January there were serious worries about the attitude of the military commanders. In the regular meetings with the NJOC they were questioning the value of proceeding with the elections. They had come to assume a dominant position in all matters of national policy and were not persuaded of the value of a peaceful settlement if it included ZANU. They were considering the option of 'returning to the war' and appealing for South African assistance. The Treasury Secretary, Mr David Young sought to persuade the commanders of the importance of working towards a genuine election. The influence of Mr Flower, Director of the Central Intelligence Organisation, was also exerted against any unconstitutional action. But General Walls was objecting violently to public statements issued from Government House. In response to movement on a considerable scale in and out of the assembly places, he instructed the Rhodesian forces to patrol nearer the assembly areas.

3. The Governor commented that in proceeding with the settlement and the elections we had to steer a difficult course between conflicting requirements. We must persuade the Rhodesian military commanders to continue to work with us toward an election to be held in conditions as acceptable to international opinion as possible; and that, whatever the outcome of the elections, this was better than a return to the war. This was the reverse of their present thinking. We must resist Rhodesian demands for the banning of ZANU. We also had to work out a viable plan for the Patriotic Front forces in the assembly areas after the elections. We were repeatedly reminded that the Rhodesians were given assurances at Lancaster House that we would not permit significant violations of the Lancaster House agreements without taking action against the party responsible for them; and that this was the condition on which the Salisbury delegation had agreed to the settlement. The great majority of breaches of the cease-fire and acts of intimidation continued to be attributable to ZANLA. The Rhodesians had produced evidence of deliberate instructions from the ZANU High Command that ZANLA units should break up into small groups or individuals, a considerable number of whom had been instructed to remain outside the assembly places. Intimidation by ZANLA was particularly severe in Victoria Province and in Manicaland. The cooler heads in the NJOC accepted that we were not going to ban ZANU; but none of them would be willing to proceed if we were not prepared to consider limited and selective action against ZANU in relation to clear breaches of the agreement. A technical problem over ZANU's participation in the election was settled early in the campaign. Rev Sithole had sought to challenge in the courts the designation ZANU-PF chosen by Mr Mugabe's party. He

wanted the title ZANU exclusively for his own party. Had this action been allowed to continue, the timetable for the elections agreed at Lancaster House might have been jeopardised. The Governor therefore enacted an ordinance staying until after the election any legal action to challenge a party's designation or election symbol.

4. On 19 January, after a long private argument, General Walls accepted that we were not going to ban ZANU and that he must do something about the South African forces. On 21 January the NJOC held a meeting to decide whether to proceed with the settlement. Mr David Young, who had consulted some of the other permanent secretaries, told the Rhodesian commanders that a refusal to do so would have disastrous consequences for Rhodesia. He was strongly supported by Mr Flower. Air Marshal McLaren was the leading advocate of a return to the war. By this time General Walls had come round to the side of the moderates. But Mr Young was sufficiently worried by the state of mind of the military commanders to have given instructions that, if they took unconstitutional action, no foreign exchange should be released to them for their military requirements. On the following day General Walls assured us that he had no intention of letting Rhodesian forces get so close to the assembly places as to cause a breakdown of the cease-fire.

5. The Governor reported that in addition to taking powers to disqualify a party in a given electoral or administrative district, he proposed to take powers to take limited action against individuals who engaged in activities involving breaches of the agreements and to ban meetings. The publication of the Ordinance would exert further pressure on all the parties to comply with the agreements and would help to maintain confidence within the country. There was general concern about intimidation, not only by ZANLA but also to a lesser extent by ZIPRA and the auxiliaries.

6. General Walls had agreed to discuss with General Malan the withdrawal of the South African elements at Beitbridge and the effective integration of South African personnel in the south east area into the Rhodesian forces. By this time Air Vice Marshal Hawkins, the Rhodesian representative in South Africa, and Mr Flower were in favour of South African withdrawal from Beitbridge. General Walls reported, however, that General Malan was strongly opposed to the integration of the South African units; no doubt General Walls did not press him very hard. By this time it was clear that the UN Security Council was likely to pass a further resolution calling for the withdrawal of the South African forces. We told General Walls that we must issue an announcement about the South African withdrawal from Beitbridge within the next few days and that other South African personnel must be integrated in the Rhodesian forces. Sir A. Duff

saw Mr P.W. Botha in Cape Town on 26 January and emphasised the danger to both Governments in relation to the Security Council debate. It was agreed to announce immediately that the South African contingent would hand over responsibility for the protection of Beitbridge to the Rhodesians. On 29 January General Walls agreed with General Malan the arrangements for the change-over at Beitbridge and that from 4 February South African and Rhodesian forces would be integrated in the south east area.

7. On 25 January General Walls and Mr Flower had a private meeting with Mr Nkomo, who complained, as he had been doing to us, about ZANLA forces who had been instructed to remain outside the assembly areas. By this time General Walls had managed to overcome resistance of the other Rhodesian commanders to the idea of trying to bring at least some ZIPRA elements into a holding unit for training purposes and that a start should be made on this before the elections. By 27 January ZANU had agreed to release the detainees in Mozambique. Mr Mugabe returned to Salisbury and addressed a meeting of 150,000 people—easily the largest of the rallies addressed by the three major political leaders.

8. On 28 January Mr Ian Smith called on the Governor to ask what he intended to do about ZANU. Mr Smith differentiated sharply between Nkomo and Mugabe. There was some discussion of the possibilities for coalitions. The Governor reported that during this conversation there were 'undertones of a white coup'.

9. On 2 February the UN Security Council passed a predictably one-sided resolution calling on Britain to ensure that no South African or other external forces remained in Rhodesia and to restrict the Rhodesian forces to their bases; and in effect calling in question the impartiality of the Governor's administration. The resolution took no account of the difficulties which had to be overcome in implementing the settlement and the large number of violations of the cease-fire by ZANLA. It was an example of the United Nations, who had no practical responsibility for the implementation of the settlement, at its worst. The British Government decided for the first time in the Security Council not to participate in the vote.

10. The Governor commented at this stage that so far we had managed with reasonable success to navigate between the reefs on which the settlement could founder. The extremely dangerous phase to assembly and disengagement of the forces had been overcome. The difficult task of bringing back first Nkomo and secondly Mugabe and beginning to integrate them and their followers into political life had been fulfilled. But the entire Rhodesian establishment, the internal parties and now—in private—Nkomo were arguing that if the present level of intimidation by ZANLA continued, it would not be possible to hold elections in the eastern provinces in which the other parties had a fair chance to compete. Nkomo had

been prevented by ZANU from holding a meeting in Umtali; Muzorewa had been prevented from addressing one in Manicaland his home area.

11. On the credit side Mr Nkomo was beginning to be accepted by the white community. Although he would complain from time to time about our administration, we had a good relationship with him. Relations with Bishop Muzorewa were at a low ebb as he tended to put the blame on us for difficulties he was experiencing in his campaign. There were hopes that the outcome of the elections might be a coalition involving Mr Nkomo, Muzorewa and the whites. This would depend on the electoral arithmetic; and Mr Nkomo would insist on the premiership. An election result which left Mugabe in a dominant position might well be resisted by the Rhodesian forces. In the next period it would be essential to the credibility of the Governor's administration to demonstrate that we were prepared to take action to deal with systematic intimidation. The Governor would be gazetting on 5 February the first Ordinance giving him powers to take selective action. He hoped that this would in itself be a deterrent. Our other main concern was the problem, on which we had so far been able to make little progress, of the future of the 22,000 armed men in the assembly areas.

12. On 3 February 18 people were killed in an attack attributed to ZANLA on a bus near Umtali. Bishop Muzorewa told the Governor that he thought he had been mistaken to sign the Lancaster House agreements. It was impossible for him or any other party except ZANU to campaign in the eastern provinces. On 5 February Mr Nkomo also said that he was concerned about intimidation throughout the eastern provinces. As he had told the press that morning, one of his candidates had been murdered by ZANLA. The Governor refused to consider postponing the elections. Mr Nkomo confirmed that he was ready to pursue some integration of ZIPRA forces; the same offer should be made to ZANLA. All ZIPRA forces would be given clear instructions to stay in the assembly areas after the elections.

13. On 4 February the repatriation of the refugees from Mozambique began at the rate of 500 a day. The return of refugees from Botswana had begun on 21 January. By the time of the elections virtually all the 20,000 refugees in Botswana had returned; and a further 15,000 refugees had returned from Zambia and Mozambique. The process of bringing back the refugees was resumed in mid-March, as soon as the country had settled down after the elections.

14. On 5 February the Governor promulgated the Ordinance giving him the power to take selective action against a party systematically in breach of the Lancaster House agreements. On 8 February the British election supervisors in the provinces reported to the Governor that in the tribal trust

lands in the eastern provinces there had been systematic intimidation by ZANU over a long period. ZANLA groups outside the assembly places were concentrating on preventing meetings by other parties and impressing on the population that if ZANU did not win the elections the war would be resumed. This was the picture throughout all of Matabeleland, Victoria Province and the rural areas of Mashonaland. Although all the Matabeleland was Nkomo territory, other parties were able to campaign. There were also accusations, some of which could be substantiated, about misbehaviour by the auxiliaries; but the overwhelming picture was one of systematic intimidation by ZANLA.

15. The Commonwealth observers had by this time arrived in Rhodesia. Apart from the Australian representative, Mr Shann, they showed little interest in ZANLA activity. They concentrated on the actions of the administration and allegations of bias against the Patriotic Front. The Governor commented that it was in fact impossible to hold completely free and fair elections with the country just emerging from a violent conflict which was continuing—albeit on a lesser scale—in the eastern districts. What we were seeking to do was to organise the freest and fairest elections it was possible to hold in the circumstances prevailing in Rhodesia.

16. On 9 February the ZANLA commander, Nhongo, was persuaded to make a broadcast calling on outstanding ZANLA forces to report to the assembly places. This produced no response. On the same day the Governor reluctantly took action under the Ordinance to prohibit a ZANU candidate (Mr Nkala) from campaigning, though not from standing, in the elections. Mr Nkala had been saying publicly that if ZANU did not win, the war would continue. The Governor reported that the presence of party agents in the polling booths could have an intimidatory effect. A British presence would be required in all the polling booths. It was subsequently agreed that 500 British policemen should be sent to Rhodesia for this purpose for the week of the elections.

17. Acts of violence and intimidation were, however, by no means confined to ZANU. On 22 December two of Mr Mugabe's nephews were injured in an attack on the house of his sister. On 5 February a ZANU candidate, Mr Kangai, was wounded in a rocket attack on his house by members of the UANC youth wing. The same group threw a grenade at Mr Mugabe's house. The police were concerned about the involvement of one of Bishop Muzorewa's sons in acts of intimidation. On 9 February Mr Garfield Todd was arrested by the police in Shabani under the Law and Order Maintenance Act because a schoolmaster on his farm had helped a member of ZANLA. The Governor secured his immediate release and the dropping of the charges against him. On 10 February Mr Mugabe was very nearly killed when, on route to the airport after addressing a political rally

in Fort Victoria, a mine was exploded by remote control in an attack on his car. On 13 February three ZANU candidates were arrested by the Shabani police. On 14 February explosions took place outside the churches in Salisbury. A lieutenant and another member of the Selous Scouts blew themselves up in a car on the same evening. The police had no doubt they had been responsible for the bombings. These attacks caused Mr Mugabe to cancel all further appearances at public meetings before the elections.

18. There continued to be strong protests from the Patriotic Front about the activities of the security force auxiliaries. There were auxiliary detachments in most of the major tribal trust lands. The Rhodesian commanders would not agree that they should be confined to barracks. This would in their view have left the tribal trust lands entirely in the hands of the guerrillas. Their activities were closely monitored by the Commonwealth force. But the 'psychological operations' branch of Combined Operations produced and distributed, without the Governor's authority, pamphlets extolling the virtues of 'true democracy' with propaganda hostile to the Patriotic Front. With characteristic incompetence bundles of these pamphlets were dropped by air on some of the Commonwealth observers.

19. In discussions with the NJOC we were intensifying our efforts to persuade the Rhodesians to accept responsibility for the assembly places as soon as the elections had been held. At this stage the military plans were still based on withdrawal of all monitoring force personnel from the assembly places on 29 February. But it was clear that this was likely to destabilise the assembly places. Mr Nkomo was anxious that the monitoring force should remain. We began to consider the possibility of leaving smaller numbers of British monitors in the assembly places in a liaison role.

20. We also sought to increase the pressure on ZANU to discontinue or reduce systematic intimidation directed against other parties—failing which Muzorewa, the Rhodesian commanders and Nkomo were all liable to contest the value of proceeding with the elections. On 12 February the Governor made a further Ordinance and we published a list of the areas in which systematic intimidation, acts of political violence and threats against voters were such that campaigning could not at present be fully undertaken. A marked improvement was looked for to enable fair elections to be held in these areas. Maps were circulated indicating the areas worst affected and those in which intimidation was taking place though on a less serious scale. The areas in question concerned in all about 20% of the voting population. The Governor prohibited further campaigning by ZANU in one area of Victoria Province affected by the continuing ZANLA activity.

21. After a series of discussions Mr Nkomo agreed that the ZIPRA battalion at assembly point Lima should be moved to a training camp outside Bulawayo, under the auspices of the monitoring force. The Rhodesians would be involved in their training. On 14th February General Acland and the Rhodesian army commander agreed with Mr Nkomo on the arrangements to bring the ZIPRA contingent under training. A similar offer was made to ZANLA. On 16th February Mr Mugabe was informed of our offer to take a ZANLA contingent to a training camp under the auspices of the monitoring force. Mr Mugabe agreed to this and to issue orders to his forces to remain in the assembly places after the elections. He regarded it as essential that the monitoring force should remain in the country after independence to provide stability, preside over the integration of the forces and train the new Zimbabwe army.

22. The Rhodesian Front won all 20 seats in the elections for the white members of parliament on 14th February. In most cases their candidates were returned unopposed. The Rhodesians continued to demand that the Governor should take action to penalise ZANU for systematic intimidation and persistent breaches of the cease-fire. The Police Commissioner produced details of areas on the north east border, the Buhera area in Manicaland and the Belingwe area in Victoria Province where violence was continuing at much the same level as before the cease-fire, where there was systematic intimidation of voters and where other parties were unable to campaign. Intimidation in the areas concerned affected 10% of the voting population. There were indications that the threat of action in some of the more 'redeemable' areas was having some effect on the ability of other parties to campaign.

23. On 19 February Mr Nkomo complained again that his party was unable to campaign in the eastern provinces. Some of his party workers had been abducted or murdered. The Governor said that any action would be bound to attract severe international criticism. How much support would we get from him? Mr Nkomo, characteristically, said that he would not make a public declaration of support but would not criticise the action we took. He was in fact looking to us to try to ensure that he won the elections, while seeking himself to avoid any involvement in the action for which he was pressing. The Governor said that apart from the international implications, there was a danger that action would push ZANLA out of the assembly places and Mozambique back into support for Mr Mugabe. Mr Nkomo said that he had made his position clear to the Commonwealth observers.

24. On 20 February General Walls suggested that he should propose to the Patriotic Front leaders that they and the Rhodesian commanders should tour the Patriotic Front assembly places together, to assure them of their

security if they remained in the assembly places after the elections. Progress was at last being made on the establishment of a permanent Rhodesian presence in the assembly areas. From 22 February the cease-fire commission began to visit the assembly areas to arrange for a permanent police presence and the introduction of Rhodesian army liaison officers.

25. On 22 February the British election supervisors and the British police and army representatives in the provinces reported to the Governor that the spreading out of the security forces, reinforced by the call up of reservists, into the tribal trust lands was helping to reduce intimidation. In some of the areas concerned other parties had now been able to address meetings. It was understood that the poll was secret. Intimidation had had its effect in many areas, but the virtually unanimous view was that this would not justify the abrogation of polling in the areas concerned.

26. On 23 February the Governor commented that the arguments against taking action against ZANU were very strong. They rested on the international reactions and the resulting consequences not only for British interests, but also on what we were seeking to achieve in Rhodesia. The comparatively small scale action we might contemplate would probably not of itself drive ZANU out of the elections; but it would greatly improve their position if they rejected the outcome. Clearly the best outcome would be to get through to the elections without having to take such action. If there was a Mugabe landslide there was a danger that the whites would react violently. Bishop Muzorewa suspected that it was our intention to install Nkomo as Prime Minister. General Walls was under strong pressure from other elements in the armed forces, who considered that he had sold Rhodesia down the river at Lancaster House. But it made little sense to take arbitrary and possibly ineffective action against ZANU. The Governor reported that we would therefore be trying in talks with individual members of the NJOC and political leaders over the weekend to convince them that the best course was to run through to the elections.

27. General Walls and Mr Flower had been invited by the Mozambique Government to visit Maputo. The meeting was arranged by Mr Honwana. The Governor's staff encouraged them to accept the invitation. They met the commander of the Mozambique forces, the Foreign Minister and others. The Mozambicans argued that Mr Mugabe was not a Marxist: why did the establishment never talk to him? General Walls described ZANLA conduct but said that he would be ready to talk to Mr Mugabe as he was to Mr Nkomo, if he would talk to the Rhodesians. The Mozambicans said that they would ensure that he did.

28. On 24 February the Governor reported that General Acland had agreed with the other Commonwealth contingents that they would withdraw from the assembly places on 3 March. The small monitoring teams

remaining in the assembly places until 8 March would be British.

29. Over the weekend Sir A. Duff and Mr Renwick talked to General Walls, Mr Young, Mr Flower and the Police Commissioner. In all cases they explained that, while a case could be made out for limited action against ZANU, if we were to abrogate or postpone polling in a limited number of areas, this undoubtedly would affect acceptance of the result both inside and outside the country. Such action would, furthermore, have very little effect on the overall result. Mr Young agreed with this analysis but was worried about the danger of hotheads in the military establishment getting out of hand. Mr Flower reported that Bishop Muzorewa was think-ing of summoning a meeting of his Lancaster House delegation to discuss whether or not to withdraw from the agreements. Both the Police Com-missioner and Mr Flower were still hankering after some action, but seemed to be wavering. General Walls did not contradict our reasoning but did not say that he accepted it. He said that Mr Nkomo was clearly looking to us to take some action but he was more worried about Bishop Muzo-rewa, who was seriously contemplating calling his government together and trying to resume control of the country. In that case he would look to the Rhodesian army to support him but, said General Walls, 'I am not sure that the Rhodesian army would support him'.

30. Apart from the efforts made to convince them that the best course was to proceed normally to the elections, the Rhodesian attitude at this stage was influenced by their forecast of the likely outcome of the elec-tions. They had no doubt that a high proportion of the population in the tribal trust lands would vote for ZANU, but believed that a majority of the people in the towns and in the European farming areas would vote for Bishop Muzorewa. While forecasting accurately the extent of Mr Nkomo's support they believed that ZANU and the Bishop's party would divide the Shona votes about equally between them. We were sceptical of the Rhodesian assessment to the extent that we shared the view of virtually all other observers that ZANU would win the largest number of seats. It did not, however, seem probable (to anyone except the Mozambicans) that ZANU would by themselves be able to win an absolute majority. No fore-cast could be based on anything other than guess-work. But the Rhodesian assessment was fortunate in that it reduced the danger of a confrontation over their demands for action against ZANU.

31. On 25 February, two days before the elections, Mr Flower told us that the NJOC had decided that morning not to seek to insist the Governor should take action against ZANU. The case against taking action was ar-gued by Mr Flower. General Walls' support was decisive in convincing his colleagues. General Walls and Mr Flower were summoned to a meet-ing with Bishop Muzorewa who had convened most of the members of his

Lancaster House delegation. The question at issue was whether they should decide that the agreement they had entered into in the London negotiations was null and void; postpone the elections; or seek in some way to re-establish the 'Government of National Unity', perhaps with the participation of Mr Nkomo. Mr Ian Smith argued that the elections should be postponed. Bishop Muzorewa and his delegation were, however, convinced by General Walls and Mr Flower that they must proceed with them. General Walls reported that his discussions with Mr Nkomo had given him the impression that he did not intend to try to re-establish an alliance only with ZANU (though there would be pressures from other African countries on him to do so). They were left with the impression that Bishop Muzorewa himself did not wish to go back on the Lancaster House agreements, but had been under pressure from his party to do so. The Governor commented that General Walls' influence appeared to have been decisive in checking any moves for denunciation of the Lancaster House agreements. The Rhodesian commanders were now firmly of the opinion that Mr Nkomo must be an important feature of the next government. We had therefore just managed to get round this corner, albeit with screaming tyres.

32. The Governor confirmed to the FCO and to the front-line States that he had decided not to make use of his powers to disqualify a party or postpone the elections in any districts, despite a good deal of intimidation by ZANLA. The decision was based on the consideration that any action of this kind was liable to be regarded as arbitrary. The Governor did not wish to give external critics and particularly the front-line Presidents, any excuse to argue that the elections were not free and fair. He believed that this decision was in the long term and wider interests of Rhodesia. On the same day we announced the move of the ZIPRA contingent from assembly point Lima to a training camp near Bulawayo and that a similar offer had been made to ZANLA. President Nyerere announced, as we expected he would, that his country would not recognise the results of the elections if the Patriotic Front failed to win them. It was clear, he said, that the results would be rigged.

33. On the 26 February the Governor told Mr Nkomo of his decision. The Governor said that he was unhappy about the way in which ZANU had conducted their campaign. But he had concluded that if he took action against them before the elections this would affect international acceptance of the result. Mr Nkomo was bitter about ZANU's conduct and was talking in terms of trying to 'win over' some elements of ZANLA. Mr Nkomo agreed that in the aftermath of the elections he and the Rhodesian army commander should both visit the ZIPRA assembly places to instruct

his forces to remain in them. On the same day we announced that following a tour of the assembly places by the cease-fire commission, a Rhodesian military police presence was being established in them, the role of the monitoring force would change to liaison and training. Two assembly places were closed with the move of ZIPRA to the training camp at Essexvale. Joint police/Patriotic Front patrols were taking place round several of the assembly areas.

34. On the eve of the elections on 26 February the Governor asked Mr Mugabe to call in a move to try to establish relations of greater confidence with him. Mr Mugabe agreed to the proposal that a contingent of his forces should move into a training camp with Rhodesian participation and, over-ruling Mr Nhongo, that they should be armed with Rhodesian weapons. He also agreed to tour the ZANLA assembly places in the period between the elections and the declaration of the results to instruct his forces to remain in them. The Governor said that he was concerned about intimidation by ZANLA but had decided that it was in Rhodesia's interest to allow the elections to go through without any move to proscribe any areas. Mr Mugabe welcomed the decision. After the elections he thought that the most natural coalition would be with Mr Nkomo, but he might invite Bishop Muzorewa and some of his supporters also to join the government. He did not want anyone to feel that they had to leave the country, but there would need to be seen to be Africanisation, particularly in the civil service. He had many anxieties about how he was going to govern. He realised he would not have many people of administrative skills around him. He regarded the most important matter after the elections as the date of independence. Independence should not be granted for many months and the Governor and his staff should stay in order to give confidence to people. The Governor told him that this was not in our minds: he did not see what role he could play once the government had been chosen and was in the saddle. But he would report these views to the British Government. On the same day, as agreed with the Mozambicans, General Walls had a meeting with Mr Mugabe. Mr Mugabe complained, though not in an aggressive manner about the deployment of the security forces, the activities of the auxiliaries, the bomb explosions in Salisbury and the attempts to assassinate him. General Walls assured Mr Mugabe that he had no knowledge of these incidents or of the bomb explosions. He also assured him that if the ZANLA forces remained in the camps the Rhodesians were not going to attack them. Mr Mugabe said that some people thought that the Rhodesian forces might stage a coup. General Walls said that they would not do so.

3. The Transition to Independence (March-April 1980)

1. On 27 February, the first day of the elections, 1,375,000 people—nearly half the total electorate—voted. General Barnard, the Rhodesian representative on the cease-fire commission, proposed that instead of continuing to attribute responsibility for breaches of the cease-fire, the commission should concentrate on positive measures to bring about reconciliation and a permanent peace. The Governor and others who visited the polling stations detected the first signs of a landslide in favour of ZANU. ZANU supporters were active and vocal in the queues outside them. It was clear that the tide was running strongly in Mr Mugabe's favour. On 28 February the UN Secretary-General's representative, Ambassador Perez de Cuellar, told the Governor that he had been extremely impressed by the conduct of the poll and disconcerted by the evident bias of some members of the Commonwealth team. By the end of the day 2,281,146 people had voted.

2. By 29 February there were many indications that the tide was running strongly in favour of Mr Mugabe in Mashonaland. Mr Nkomo seemed certain to sweep Matabeleland but was having difficulty in attracting support elsewhere. By the end of the three-day election 2, 699,450 people out of an estimated electorate of 2.8 to 2.9 millions had voted. The British election supervisors reported evidence of intimidation by ZANLA in some areas of Victoria, Midlands and Mashonaland East provinces; but over by far the greater part of the country voting had taken place in normal conditions. General Walls revealed that he had been under pressure from some sections of the Rhodesian Front to take military action. He had rejected this and was also resisting pressure from some sections of the armed forces. The Rhodesian commanders were very concerned about indications that ZANU were building up a considerable lead, though no-one believed at this stage that they would win over 50 seats. On 1 March General Walls and Mr Flower told Bishop Muzorewa that preliminary reports suggested that ZANU were going to get a large number of seats. They proposed a coalition between Bishop Muzorewa, Mr Nkomo and the whites and told Bishop Muzorewa that it was unlikely that Mr Nkomo would agree to participate in such a coalition except as Prime Minister.

3. General Walls told us that he had sent a message to the Prime Minister, seeking reassurance that our objective was to avoid a marxist-dominated government. He had been told formally by the Joint Operations Commands in the eastern areas that they did not accept that the elections in those areas were free and fair owing to extensive intimidation. He was trying to hold the army in line. The provincial commanders had recommended that if the elections produced a Mugabe landslide and this was not accepted by the other parties, there should be an interim Council of State

representing the four major parties under the Governor. The Governor commented that to avoid the dangers of a coup, we must go on working to bring Muzorewa, Nkomo and the whites together before the results were announced; but must seek also to ensure that an offer was made to ZANU. Any attempt to exclude ZANU would be bound to result in a resumption of the war. The Rhodesians at this stage were still not reconciled to ZANU's participation. Over the weekend Mr Nkomo toured the ZIPRA and Mr Muzenda the ZANLA assembly places to instruct their forces to remain in them and to explain the arrangements for the phased withdrawal of the monitoring force. Mr Mugabe had left for Mozambique during the elections, returning to Salisbury on 2 March.

4. The Governor had requested all the observer groups present at the elections to state before the results were known whether they regarded them as having been free and fair. By 3 March the great majority of the observer groups, including the British parliamentary and official observers, the observer teams from most other western countries and the Commonwealth observers, had made public their conclusions that the elections would reflect the wishes of the people of Rhodesia.

5. Sir A. Duff and Mr Renwick saw the NJOC at their request that morning. The Rhodesian commanders stated their wish to record that they did not regard the elections as free and fair. Sir A. Duff made it clear that while Sir John Boynton's preliminary report would acknowledge that the results had been distorted by intimidation in some areas, it would conclude that the overall result of the poll reflected the wishes of the people of Rhodesia. The NJOC expressed their concern that if ZANU won an overall majority there would be a period of chaos and a mass exodus of whites. They sought to open up the possibility of our continuing to play a role and independence being deferred. Before a further meeting with the NJOC in the evening, Sir A. Duff told General Walls, in response to his message to the Prime Minister, that there could be no question of invalidating the election results.

6. At the further meeting, the NJOC said that on their advice the Muzorewa Government had been persuaded to accept the Lancaster House agreement. There had been extensive intimidation before and during the elections about which a mass of evidence had been provided. Some expressed regret that they had embarked on a course which had led to this result, though others had the grace to admit that they could not have won the war in any event. It was argued strongly that we could not walk away from the outcome. If the NJOC were to resign themselves to the result, it would be essential for us to help mitigate the effects of the transition. This could only be done if we were prepared to continue to play a role for some time which would offer the possibility for those who wished to leave the

country of being able to do so in an orderly manner; reassure the African population, including African members of the security forces; and provide a presence during the process of integration of the armed forces. There were further strong pleas for assistance with the pensions of public servants or at least action to encourage them to stay. The senior echelons of the public service were liable to melt away unless some action was taken. Sir A. Duff gave no encouragement to believe that we would be able to help over pensions. We would be aiming to achieve as broadly based a government as possible and were ready to help in whatever way we could during the transition to independence.

7. By this time it was clear that ZANU had won 57 seats. Bishop Muzorewa had won only 3. Mr Nkomo was severely shaken by the outcome and that fact that the 20 seats he had won corresponded precisely to the extent of Ndebele support. Despite one or two references to the possibility of unconstitutional action, we judged that the Rhodesian commanders were now convinced of the madness of such a course and that they would not get South African support for it; and that they would do their best to keep their subordinates in check. General Walls had a meeting with the provincial commanders on 2 March at which, after much wild talk, they had agreed on this. He took the other commanders to see Mr Mugabe on the afternoon of 3 March to exchange mutual assurances; and went on television that evening to make a statement about the need to accept the election results calmly.

8. There was no doubt, however, about the severity of the shock which would be felt on the following day by the white community, the security forces and Nkomo's supporters. The Governor considered that we must help to ease the transition towards independence, though in doing so we should not saddle ourselves with an open-ended commitment. Mr Mugabe's landslide victory posed the problem that, although he had won the support of virtually the whole of the Shona-speaking population, he had no support in Matabeleland or with the whites. Mr Nkomo had won the entire Ndebele vote, had 6,000 armed men inside the country and another 8,000 or more in Zambia. The Rhodesian forces remained intact and were undefeated. Our task over the next few days would be to damp down the reactions, to begin to assist Mr Mugabe into the process of government and to prevail on him to see the need to accommodate his political opponents and to achieve a *modus vivendi* with the security force commanders and others. General Walls was exercising his authority against a coup, but if Mr Mugabe wished to consolidate his government and to prevent the administration disintegrating it would be essential to make some offer to the white community which would reassure them, including bringing someone like Mr David Smith into his government.

9. The Governor saw Mr Mugabe on 4 March and asked him to form a government. Mr Mugabe said that he intended to include Mr Nkomo and possibly one or two members of the white community. Through Mr Honwana we had already put to Mr Mugabe the need to ask General Walls to take charge of the integration of the three armies as the best way to ease the transitional process, damp down reactions in the Rhodesian armed forces and retain white confidence. Mr Mugabe had said that he would be asking for British military instructors to help with this process, as well as for assistance with the new Zimbabwe civil service. Mr Mugabe expressed appreciation of the role the Governor had played and hoped that he would stay until the anxieties of the white population were allayed and they were confident that their interests would be protected. The Governor said that the processes leading to independence would be spread out over a few weeks. Over the next few days we would be able to assess the mood of the country and take a view on the best timing for independence. Mr Mugabe agreed to make a broadcast that evening as Prime Minister-designate. He asked what the Governor saw as the important points to make; the Governor gave him some notes. When the Governor saw Mr Nkomo later in the morning he told him that his participation in the government was essential for the future of Zimbabwe. Mr Nkomo agreed that he must accept the result and participate in the government.

10. General Walls told us that he was continuing to resist pressures to take action to prevent a Mugabe-led government being installed. We had a responsibility to help to ensure an orderly transition, to reduce the danger of conflict breaking out again and to ensure that the inevitable white exodus was as orderly as possible. We said that we could not prolong our direct responsibility. The Governor could not stay with no real authority, but we had no intention of rushing through the constitutional processes. We would try to assist in the period after independence with a military training scheme. General Walls' personal distress was very great. We pointed out that it had been our assessment, before the negotiations began, that the war was not winnable from the Rhodesian point of view. The Patriotic Front could not defeat the Rhodesian armed forces, but within a year or two at the most they would have worn down the white community generally sufficiently to provoke some kind of collapse. Nor was it possible to explain the extent of Mr Mugabe's electoral victory by intimidation. Virtually the entire Shona-speaking population had voted for him. Any attempt to seek to frustrate the result by military action would be disastrous. General Walls said that he accepted this though some elements of the army did not.

11. The Governor commented that both Mr Mugabe and General Walls were asking us to continue to play a role. We must be prepared to assist

the new government. What we had set out to do was to bring Zimbabwe to independence, if possible with a government open to the West. The received wisdom had been that a Mugabe government would be a disaster in this respect. The Governor did not agree that this would necessarily be the case. He was more worried about the people around Mr Mugabe than about him. If we failed to help in the early days of his government, we should force him to look elsewhere.

12. In the evening Mr Mugabe made an eloquent and statesmanlike broadcast. He confirmed that Mr Nkomo would be asked to join his government as would representatives of other communities. His government would adhere to the constitution and obey the rule of law, upholding fundamental human rights. It was not his intention to interfere with pension or individual property rights. He would authorise General Walls, working with the ZANLA and ZIPRA commanders, to preside over the integration of the armed forces. They would continue to enjoy the assistance of British military instructors. His government would strive to bring about meaningful change, but this could not occur overnight.

13. On 6 March Mr Mugabe told the Governor that he would want to apply for membership of the Commonwealth. On the following day we made a public statement that our purpose was to achieve an orderly transfer of power to the elected government and that we would proceed deliberately towards independence. Britain would be ready to continue its assistance to Zimbabwe after independence, including the services of a British military training team.

14. The Governor told Mr Mugabe on 10 March that we were aiming for independence at the end of the month. Mr Mugabe asked the Governor to reconsider this. He was concerned that independence should not be rushed. He valued the Governor's advice in this crucial period. It was important to him to be able to talk in confidence to someone with wide experience of government. His team were not ready to be rushed into government. He had only suggested that independence should be granted at the end of April because he knew that we would not be prepared to stay longer. He would himself have preferred us to do so. The Governor said that, so long as he remained in Rhodesia, there could not be a conflict of authority. We were concerned about the difficulties which could arise in too protracted an interim, with Ministers wanting to initiate new policies and becoming frustrated because authority remained with the Governor. Mr Mugabe said that on the time scale we envisaged, this would not arise. He would see to it that his Ministers understood the position and would not take initiatives which would embarrass us. The Governor concluded that we must set a term on our involvement, but should be prepared to stay

until 18 April. In this period he would remain responsible for the government. The new Ministers would familiarise themselves with the work of their departments. These arrangements were far from ideal but offered the best chance of achieving peaceful transition and giving the country the best possible start.

15. Mr Mugabe had several discussions with the Governor on the formation of his government. He was conscious of the need to make appointments which would help to retain the confidence of the white community. In the light of these discussions he decided to appoint Mr David Smith Minister of Commerce and Industry and the President of the Farmers Union, Mr Denis Norman, Minister of Agriculture. The list of Ministers was finalised after a meeting between the Government and Mr Mugabe on 11 March. Mr Nkomo agreed to participate in the government as Minister for Home Affairs. His party were given three other minor posts in the Cabinet; not surprisingly they were dissatisfied with the allocation of portfolios. The Governor commented that the government was as well balanced as we could have hoped for in the circumstances. It was encouraging that the moderate Mr Muzenda had become Minister for Foreign Affairs. The return of Mr Chidzero from the United Nations as Planning Minister would strengthen Mr Mugabe's weak economic team. Mr Mugabe had been ready to seek advice and to exert his own increased authority within the ZANU Central Committee to achieve this result.

16. On 12 March the Governor reported that most whites who had initially been stunned by Mr Mugabe's landslide victory were adopting a 'wait and see' attitude. There had not been any sudden exodus but there were disturbing indications that a considerable proportion of whites in the army and police might leave at the end of April, when they would be able to commute their pensions. The private sector were behaving sensibly, but whites in the public service doubted if they had any future. It was important to try to persuade a fair number of them to stay, so that the inevitable run-down in the numbers of the white community would take place gradually and without excessive disruption of the economy and the administration.

17. In a further talk with Mr Mugabe on 13 March it was agreed that Zimbabwe should become independent at midnight on 17/18 April. The Governor decided to return to London to discuss the way ahead and assistance to Zimbabwe with his Cabinet colleagues on 17 March. In preparation for these meetings he sent his advice on further policy. He understood the concern felt in London that we should be cautious about getting involved in the enormous problems which would confront the new government. But in view of our interests in Zimbabwe and the general problems confronting southern Africa, it was of great importance to establish the

best relationship we could with it; to take advantage of the opportunity to influence its policies; and to try to steer it away from actions likely to upset the apple cart in Rhodesia or leading to an early confrontation with South Africa. Mr Mugabe had made it clear that he wanted military assistance to come from Britain rather than elsewhere. The Director of Military Assistance in the Ministry of Defence, General Perkins, had already identified a need for assistance on a considerable scale. The exodus of Rhodesian officers and NCOs would increase the need for help in training the new army.

18. The Governor considered that we could not afford to move at a deliberate pace in deciding our aid commitment. The new government would have to embark on a massive resettlement and reconstruction programme. The country had an effective administration machine and considerable resources. But the needs would be great in the short term. We should set in train an international appeal for aid to the new State. A donors' conference would have to be organised after independence. We should encourage Zimbabwe to join the Lomé Convention. We must also consider urgently what we could do to try to encourage a reasonable proportion of the whites in the army, police and especially the civil service to stay. If there were a massive exodus this would have an effect on the economy and administration which could negate the effect of development aid. We should assist with advice on the organisation of the civil service and the new Foreign Ministry. If we made this effort, the risks of Zimbabwe taking a downward path would be reduced. We should not commit ourselves to massive programmes of indefinite duration but ought to complete the task we had undertaken at Lancaster House. If we took the lead in a generous manner and promptly we should be able to persuade others to follow. After the achievements of the last seven months, we should not throw away this opportunity. 'Let us do it with some style and ungrudgingly'.

19. On his return to Salisbury on 20 March the Governor was able to tell Mr Mugabe that he had secured his colleagues' agreement to providing an immediate grant of £7m for assistance with reconstruction. There would also be generous development aid over the next three years. We would be seeking to persuade others to follow our example. We would provide military and police assistance, advice to the civil service and on broadcasting. Mr Mugabe expressed his gratitude in a letter to the Prime Minister. He told the Governor that he had no intention of becoming beholden to the Soviet Union. The Russians had never provided him with arms. He owed them nothing. He rejected a proposal that the Russian Deputy Foreign Minister should visit Salisbury before independence.

20. By this time it had been possible to put an end to what remained of the martial law legislation. For the future much would depend on progress

with the integration of the armies. The military integration committee under General Walls ran into serious difficulties, with the ZANLA representatives resisting the demobilisation of any ZANLA forces. There were by now over 20,000 ZANLA in the assembly places. General Walls was pressing ahead with arrangements to demobilise the auxiliaries, district security assistants and farm militia (some 25,000 men) and the abolition of the call-up for white reservists. The ZIPRA commanders were reacting to the ZANLA attitude. Considerable difficulties had to be overcome over the return of ZIPRA from Zambia. General Fursdon arrived to make recommendations on the military assistance we should provide.

21. On 24 March the Governor visited Mozambique at the invitation of President Machel. The President expressed his appreciation of the steps Lord Soames and the British Government had taken to bring Rhodesia to independence. The settlement would bring great benefit to Mozambique. The Mozambicans hoped that we would be able to assist with agricultural development and with the rehabilitation of road and rail communications with Rhodesia and the port of Beira. The Mozambican representative in Salisbury, Mr Honwana, had done much to help while the settlement was being put into effect. The Governor commented that we should seek to exploit the opportunity created by the Rhodesian settlement for Britain and the West to establish a better relationship with Mozambique.

22. In response to an outbreak of disturbances in the Salisbury area, some of them inspired by local ZANU activists, Mr Mugabe told the Governor that he had no intention of allowing the situation to get out of control. On 25 March he made a broadcast emphasizing his determination to avoid any breakdown of law and order. No-one, he said, was blameless, least of all members of his own party. To reassure the civil service, Mr Mugabe gave a further assurance that pension rights would be honoured. Invitations were issued to over one hundred governments to send delegations to the independence celebrations. Mr Mugabe told the Governor that he would wish to invite the liberation movements (ANC, PAC, SWAPO, PLO and POLISARIO). It was agreed that they should be invited by the party rather than the government.

23. On 27 March Mr Mugabe wrote a letter undertaking to honour the debts contracted to the United Kingdom, before the illegal declaration of independence, enabling ECGD cover to be extended to Zimbabwe. Mr David Young told us that following talks which he and Mr David Smith had with Mr Mugabe's authority in South Africa, the South Africans were considering whether to make available soft loans worth 165 million rand which had provisionally been allocated to Rhodesia. The South Africans were concerned about the possible use of Zimbabwe territory by the

SAANC and the future of their mission in Salisbury. The Governor commented that Mr Mugabe had made it clear that it would not be possible for this government to 'fight South Africa' and that the preservation of economic links with South Africa was essential. He had not yet come to any conclusion about the future of the diplomatic mission but might be prepared to turn it into a trade office. But he would certainly continue to attack apartheid.

24. On 31 March the Governor reported that there were now 29,000 men in the assembly places; 6-7,000 outstanding ZANLA had reported to them since the elections. Although a system of resettlement grants had been worked out, in view of the resistance of the Patriotic Front commanders it had not been possible to make significant progress with demobilisation. The Joint Operations Commands had been dissolved. The police were now responsible for internal security though they could request the assistance of the army when necessary. We were working on the setting up of a Joint Military High Command.

25. On 1 April Mr Mugabe attended a conference of the front-line States in Lusaka. On his return the South African diplomatic representative told him that he was being recalled while the future character of official relations between the two states was agreed. The South Africans were upset at the failure to invite them to the independence celebrations and the decision to invite the liberation movements. Mr Mugabe told the Governor that in Lusaka he had told the ANC that they could not have any military bases in Zimbabwe. He would support them in international conferences, but not militarily. The Governor told the South African diplomatic representative that in the aftermath of the elections we were doing all we could to help stabilise the situation. If the South Africans themselves began to take actions which undermined white confidence or pressed the new government too hard politically, they were liable to exacerbate the dangers we were seeking to contain. The Governor commented that we must try to get across to the South Africans the need to show some finesse in dealing with the new government and some understanding of its problems. Mr Mugabe subsequently told the government that he had told the South Africans in good faith that there were no armed SAANC in Zimbabwe. He had since discovered that there were 87 with the ZIPRA forces. These were being returned to Zambia.

26. At the Governor's invitation, M. Cheysson, the European Commissioner for Overseas Co-operation, visited Salisbury on 1-2 April. He was impressed by the pragmatism of the new government, the quality of the civil service, the underlying resource strength of the economy (including the sound financial position in terms of external indebtedness) and the

peacefulness of the country. Mr Mugabe confirmed that he wanted Zimbabwe to join the Lomé Convention.

27. We had encouraged the withdrawal of the police from the Combined Operations structure and the abolition of the Joint Operations Commands as part of the general process of normalisation. General Walls' continued involvement for some time at least in the integration of the armed forces remained very important to the chances of success. But with the disappearance of Combined Operations headquarters, he was left with no authority vis-à-vis the other commanders. If General Walls withdrew, the tensions between ZIPRA and ZANLA would be exacerbated. On 3 April the Governor reported that he had discussed the situation with Mr Mugabe and with General Walls. Mr Mugabe agreed that General Walls must be given the necessary authority. There was an equally pressing need to give the Patriotic Front commanders status by the creation of a Joint Military High Command. At Mr Mugabe's request the Governor gave him a draft letter setting out these arrangements.

28. Mr Nkomo remained very upset about his lack of success in the elections, the allocation of portfolios in the government and the further humiliation inflicted on him when ZANU refused to permit the election of most of his candidates for the Senate. We were determined to try to recover as many as possible of the ZIPRA forces in Zambia before independence. When ZANU proposed that ZIPRA should return without their arms, Mr Nkomo refused to instruct his forces to return. The ZIPRA commanders threatened to withdraw from the military committee if this was insisted on. We agreed with General Walls that ZIPRA should be permitted to return with their small arms; but their heavy weapons must be handed over to the government or to the Zambians. On 8 April Mr Mugabe confirmed that he would give General Walls a letter giving him authority vis-à-vis the other commanders to supervise the amalgamation process and deal with other matters concerning the future of the forces. General Walls made it clear that he was only prepared to accept the commitment for a limited period and if in fact it was possible for him to make progress with the integration and demobilisation of the forces.

29. A British civil service team was advising the Minister for the Public Service, Mr Hove, and the Rhodesian public service commission on the difficult and important problem of trying to reconcile Africanisation with the need to retain the skills of many white civil servants. A high proportion of the white members of the security forces and 20% of the whites in the police force had already applied to leave. The Governor commented that there could be no question of our guaranteeing Rhodesian pensions. But if we did not take some steps to tackle this problem we could find ourselves pouring money into development projects so ill-administered as to render

our assistance largely ineffective. General Fursdon would be making recommendations in due course about military aid; but both sides were appealing to us and it was clear that this would need to be substantial.

30. On 11 April the Reverend Canaan Banana was elected President. Mr Garfield Todd was nominated to the Senate. The Patriotic Front and Rhodesian commanders and General Fursdon moved into the new joint military headquarters. Mr Nkomo was still threatening to withdraw from the government. By this time, however, arrangements had been made for nearly 8,000 ZIPRA personnel to return from Zambia with their personal arms before independence.

31. On 14 April the Governor made a farewell broadcast. On the following day the Government announced its intention to make £75 million of development aid available to Zimbabwe over the next three years.

32. On 16 April HRH The Prince of Wales arrived in Salisbury to represent The Queen at the independence celebrations. He was greeted by the Governor, the Police Commissioner, General Walls and the ZANLA and ZIPRA commanders. On the following day he visited the camp near Bulawayo at which Patriotic Front forces were training with Rhodesian personnel. In his independence message to the people of Zimbabwe Mr Mugabe paid tribute to Lord Soames for the role he had played in guiding the country through elections to independence. 'His was from the very outset a difficult and most unenviable task. . . . I am personally indebted to him for the advice he has given me on the art of managing the affairs of government.' Mr Mugabe would, he said, be missing a good friend and counsellor and so would the people of Zimbabwe. The country was brought to Independence at midnight in a ceremony attended by the Prince of Wales and delegations from over one hundred governments, with the participation of contingents from ZANLA, ZIPRA and the Rhodesian forces. On the following day the Governor and his staff left Salisbury on the completion of his mission.

British Documents from the Archives

No. 1   Britain and the making of the Post-War World: The Potsdam Conference and beyond

No. 2   Preparing for Helsinki: The CSCE Multilateral Preparatory Talks

No. 3   Britain and the Berlin Crisis, 1961

No. 4   The Rhodesia Settlement, 1979-1980: An In-House Study

Also available online: www.issuu.com/fcohistorians

Printed in Great Britain
by Amazon

35188574R00096